AN INTRODUCTION TO MUSIC

THE MACMILLAN COMPANY
NEW YORK • CHICAGO
DALLAS • ATLANTA • SAN FRANCISCO
LONDON • MANILA

IN CANADA
BRETT-MACMILLAN LTD.
GALT, ONTARIO

Robert Lilienfeld

AN INTRODUCTION TO MUSIC

New York
The Macmillan Company
1962

First Printing

The Macmillan Company, New York
Brett-Macmillan Ltd., Galt, Ontario

Printed in thre United States of America

Library of Congress catalog card number: 61-12701

ACKNOWLEDGMENTS

My thanks are due to my wife Louise, and to Frank Levy for a long series of helpful comments and discussions concerning this book, and especially to Hugo Kauder, without whose suggestions and teaching the proportion of sense to nonsense in the book would be much smaller; also to Mary Capouya for typing and painstakingly proofreading a major portion of the book, and to Emile Capouya for his long and patient wait while the book took shape.

Acknowledgments are due to the following publishers for permission to make the quotations mentioned: Alfred A. Knopf, Inc., for quotations from *The Art of Judging Music* by Virgil Thomson; J. B. Lippincott Co., *Worlds of Music* by Cecil Smith; W. W. Norton & Company, Inc., quotations from *The Bach Reader* by Hans T. David and Arthur Mendel; Pantheon Books, Inc., the passage from Schelling's essay, translated by Michael Bullock, in *The True Voice of Feeling* by Herbert Read; St Martin's Press, Inc., Athanasius Kircher's "Arca Musarithmica" in George Grove, *Dictionary of Music and Musicians.*

TO
LOUISE

CONTENTS

Introduction

Music once held an honored place in the Liberal Arts curriculum. That is to say, it was considered one of those subjects that have a universal significance, and which therefore form the basis of all education. The seven Liberal Arts—grammar, rhetoric and dialectic, music, arithmetic, astronomy, and geometry—were the basis upon which any further education, personal, specialized, or vocational, was built.

But music has somehow fallen out of our education. A good musical education, whether for the specialist or for the layman, is hardly to be found in our schools and colleges.

Most people discover, sooner or later, that their education has left them rather at a loss with respect to musical matters. The person who turns to this book is most likely one who has discovered this lack in his schooling. He will find the library shelves crowded with such books, but whether he works his way through one or a dozen of them, he is likely to find himself no better off than before. Not that books on music have nothing to say—they often contain many observations that are excellent, or at least correct. Rather it is that such observations as books have to make, true as they may be, simply do not help the listener. A book may discuss music in a variety of terms: historical, emotional, aesthetic or philosophical; or it may seek to explain music in social, biographical, or psychological terms. These are all translations of music into something else, and whatever merit a translation may possess, it does not help the reader penetrate into the original language. Even those discussions of the technical side of music which are correct from a formal, analytical point of view are no help to the listener; they burden the reader with mere information: secondhand knowledge based upon the insights or perceptions of someone else. Direct contact with music is irreducible to formulations in words.

The weakness of such approaches is that of one-sidedness; in addition to the intellectual roots of music, it must be emphasized that music also has organic roots. Its rhythms have connection with the bodily rhythms of breathing and walking, its tensions and resolutions to muscular activity and to the experience of gravity—that most primitive of the senses. By lending himself to these experiences through practical music making, the listener acquires a much more vitalized grasp of music than can ever be gained by mere reading or passive listening.

In any other age but the present, no one would have dreamed of a book explaining music. Throughout the whole life of mankind, music has been something that everyone knew how to make from his youngest years; a person no sooner expected to learn music from a book than he would have expected to learn how to breathe or use his limbs from so artificial a source. This spontaneous musical life is what we now call "folk music," and we have learned to look down upon it somewhat. But what we know as folk music is not authentic, ruined as it has been by the stream of manufactured music which for almost two centuries has replaced it. It was once something very great, both a source and an expression of vitality, and very closely akin to its brother, our "art music." Each, in fact, has taken much from the other over the centuries, with mutual benefit, but they are not one and the same. Folk music was, we have said, our spontaneous musical life; art music is something more. Intellectual values have entered into the latter—not in the sense of something very formidable and technical, but rather in the role of thought working not in opposition to feeling but in harmony with it, creating, by insight into nature and by the methods of nature, works of lasting significance.

Both these forms of musical life have become a closed book for most people. The passive indifference fostered by manufactured music—what is called popular music—has cut most people off from the real thing, to the extent that they really have lost the use of their musical faculties. Folk music is almost completely decayed, and although there have been eras when people were in close contact with the best art music of their time, this is not one of those eras. The passivity of our musical public finds expression among educated persons in the belief that music is something literary, something about which one can acquire information without direct participation or experience.

Thus a mere book may, after all, have something useful to say about rectifying musical life. This one is intended primarily for people who are not musicians, and who have had no specific musical training. I hope that it will also be helpful to those intending to embark upon a musical career, or at least a musical education. It cannot take the place of any practical work or study, and much of it may require practical work or experience to be comprehensible. Therefore it offers relatively few details of music history or theory, and burdens the reader with as few technicalities as are necessary for explaining the matter at hand. What it does hope to offer is some orientation toward the human and intellectual contexts in which a healthy musical life is lived.

Part One

THE FOUNDATIONS OF MUSIC

CHAPTER 1

Sound as Artistic Matter

Music is that art which uses sound as its material. But sound is a strange kind of "matter"; hardly has it been evoked than it dies away and disappears. The materials of all the other arts are much solider, more enduring, yet we all feel that musical creations are enduring structures, in some sense, and that music is an architecture, perhaps not material, but intellectual. In what way can such evanescent material be used?

The Impact of Sound on the Ear

The region of sound is a continual flow of sense impressions. Sounds originating on all sides of us tend to merge into one single stream; they come from all directions, but their sounds blend into one "concert" of noise. By remembering where we are, we sort out one or another sequence of noises to which our attention is directed, while leaving the rest in the background, and connect it with the events going on about us: the ticking of a clock in this room, the typewriter in the next, the hum of conversations, the footsteps above, and the motor in the street.

Noises are, in some basic sense, irregular, either in the quality of the sound, its production, or its duration. They have an accidental character. Most of the objects we hear in everyday life generate sounds only incidentally to their operation; in most cases the sounds are not particularly welcome, and objects are silenced or softened as much as possible. Even in everyday human speech we are not concerned with the sounds themselves, but rather with what is conveyed: messages, requests, information. The stream of sound in everyday life exists as a source in about equal parts of physical orientation, practical information, and of simple distraction and annoyance.

On the other hand there is also an art of sound, an activity in which sounds are employed for their own sake, and there is a rather large class of objects specifically made to produce them. The sounds generated by musical instruments are clearly quite different from those generated incidentally by doors slamming, typewriters, and so on, and we immediately respond to them as such. For one thing, they are clearly produced for their own sake. They have qualities of pitch, sonority, and pungency which have been carefully "distilled"; all distracting noises—unwanted thumps, rattles, scrapes, and so on, incidental to the production of these sounds—are softened or eliminated.

The sounds of musical instruments are beautiful and striking in their own right. The sounds of an orchestra warming up before the conductor has appeared are just as stirring and exciting in terms of pure sensation as those made after he appears. Music can be enjoyed entirely for its sensory force and richness without ever penetrating to whatever intellectual values are in some way or other tied up with the sounds. Just on this purely sensory level, musical sounds afford strong emotional and nervous stimulation. In distinction to the noises of practical life, they are produced to resound, to project a definite pitch and sonority. Even the noisemakers among the musical instruments—drums, cymbals, etc.—are made to produce some selected timbre.

In contrast to mere noises, musical tones are regular, simple, and sustained in character, obviously produced as a purpose in themselves. But musical art is not achieved simply by sounding tones together or in succession; what goes on after the conductor appears is, after all, more significant than what happens before. Even on the purely sensory level, we notice that the material of the composition is in some way coherent. The sounds are not merely "put together" (that is "composed"); they "hang together" as part of a unified substance. The more we listen to the chaos of sound, the more does it begin to take shape and focus; we begin to recognize events and outlines. We begin to glimpse the over-all form of the work, and to place its details within their context. As we do so, our feeling for form as something spatial begins to operate in the region of sound, and we begin to interpret our experiences in a spatial sense; that is to say, we feel music to be a kind of architecture in which tones are placed like building blocks in space.

TONAL SPACE

Music is a kind of architecture; we listen to compositions as if they were spatial structures which gradually unfold to our view. Of course, only a small part of the structure is exhibited as it unfolds, but we certainly feel that it is all there, beyond our limited view of it.

Strictly speaking, the region of sound is not a space, but simply a flow of sense impressions. But it has all the properties that enable the mind to interpret it in a spatial way: it is normally empty (that is, silent—the occurrence of a tone indicates the expenditure of energy); it may be occupied by "objects" (tones); the objects clash or blend, are subject to movement and change, and to all manner of variation in such properties as brightness, weight, rapidity of motion, and so on.

Tonal space even has three dimensions. First of all, we hear tones as *high or low.* Rapid vibrations generate tones that are thin, bright, tense in character; these we call high notes. Slower vibrations produce tones that are thicker, darker, more slack in character: these we call low notes. Anyone who sings the scale going upwards feels the increasing muscular tension, and the tones rising in the chest, as a struggle "uphill"—against gravity, while singing the scale downwards produces a progressive relaxation in the muscles which is experienced as a movement "downhill"—with gravity.

It is our most primitive sense for orientation in the physical world, that of the pull of gravity, which causes us to interpret sounds as occurring in a spatial dimension of high and low. In fact, it is this analogy between tonal space and physical space which makes our musical notation possible: what we hear as high or low in tonal space is seen as correspondingly high or low on the musical staff.

One might consider the second dimension of tonal space to be that of depth: *near or far,* a sense provided by the relative loudness of tones. Louder tones seem more in the foreground, just as bright lights seem closer than dim ones.

And, finally, music moves in a third dimension of its own, that of musical time; it is, however, not quite the same as physical time. For one thing, it moves at varying speeds—in one composition slowly, in another, rapidly. It may even repeat itself. And musical time is somewhat elastic: within certain limits, a given piece of music may be played at somewhat different speeds by different musicians without in any way affecting the adequacy of the performance. (But there are limits, beyond which the music is felt to be distorted. Musical time is not mechanical, like the ticking of a clock, but is more related to the pulse beat of our organism. It may speed up or slow down to some extent and still be normal.)

The materials of musical architecture are also spatial; they are what in music are called *intervals.* An interval is the result of two tones being sounded together. It is a definite form in its own right, independent of the tones that serve to materialize it, and we recognize it as such.

Each interval is a unique shape because it represents a specific *ratio* (or *proportion*). When two notes are produced simultaneously with a given ratio between their vibration frequencies, a specific interval is heard. Thus, the tones A and E express the ratio 2/3, as do also the tones G and D, and many other combinations; they are all instances of *one* musical interval, called by musicians the *perfect fifth.*

Every musical interval is the sounding of a number or proportion, and we see that tones are musical *because* they materialize numerical values—proportions. Music is the art of number and of proportion. Even noises may become a part of music by expressing simple numbers; that is, by occurring as part of a regular rhythm.

The region of sound, then, is a space filled by forms which are themselves spatial shapes, musical intervals. The intervals are numbers and proportions, which organize raw matter—sounds and tones—in recognizable, basic forms. And the craft of music consists of combining and building specific forms out of these basic forms.

CHAPTER 2

The Acoustical Foundations of Music

Frequency and Pitch

Every musical tone has two essential qualities with which we shall be concerned, qualities which depend upon the kind of vibration that produces the tone. The first is that of *pitch;* that which gives a tone its fixed place, high or low, in the acoustical range. The second is that of tone color, or *timbre.* Middle C sounded on a violin or on an oboe will have the same pitch but a different character; it is the timbre that is different.

The fixed pitch of a tone depends upon regularity of vibration; a given tone is sustained by a stable rate of vibration. Thus, a scientist will say that the tone A is produced by 440 cycles of vibration per second. A change in the rate of vibration results in a change of pitch, the higher the rate, the higher the tone. The range of audibility for the human ear is from about 16 cycles per second at one end to about 20,000 at the other. Beyond these limits we hear no sound at all, although some animals are known to respond to sounds in the region above 20,000 cycles.

Musical practice makes use of a quite narrow part of the whole range of audible frequencies; the piano keyboard covers a range of from about 27 cycles to just over 4000, and there are relatively few pieces of music which exceed this range. It is true, however, that the range of vibrations between 4000 and 10,000 cycles, though not represented by written notes, plays an important part in contributing, by way of overtones, to the tone color of musical instruments. Even so, music uses only a part of what is made available by nature.

The rate at which an object will vibrate depends mostly on its mass; larger, heavier objects tend to vibrate more slowly than do lighter, smaller ones. In fact, the relation is very precise: one half of a string length vibrates twice as fast as does the full string; one third vibrates at three times the frequency of the full string, and so on; this is termed the reciprocal relation between mass and frequency.

TONE COLOR AND OVERTONES

The different tone colors of musical instruments are an expression of not one simple type of vibration, but of complexes of vibration. This may be demonstrated by the phenomenon of the overtones.

If we set a string in vibration, it may vibrate as a simple unit: . The ends of the string are termed *nodes,* or points of rest, and the center of the string is termed a *loop,* or point of motion. Only one tone is produced. Such a simple form of vibration is in practice rather rare, and usually needs a laboratory device for its production. A tuning fork is one instrument whose vibration is fairly close to this form.

If we touch the string lightly in the center, another node-and-loop formation is induced:  . The string continues to vibrate as a tonal unit, and produces the same tone, but overlaid upon its total vibration is a faint wave of partial vibrations —each half of the string vibrating at twice the frequency of the fundamental tone. Thus, a very faint overtone is added to the fundamental.

Similarly, the string may be induced to divide into thirds:

with each third vibrating at three times the frequency of the fundamental, consequently adding another faint overtone.

The significance of these node-and-loop formations, and the overtones they produce, is that they do not have to be induced; they occur as natural phenomena in all musical instruments, in a definite pattern, following the number series.

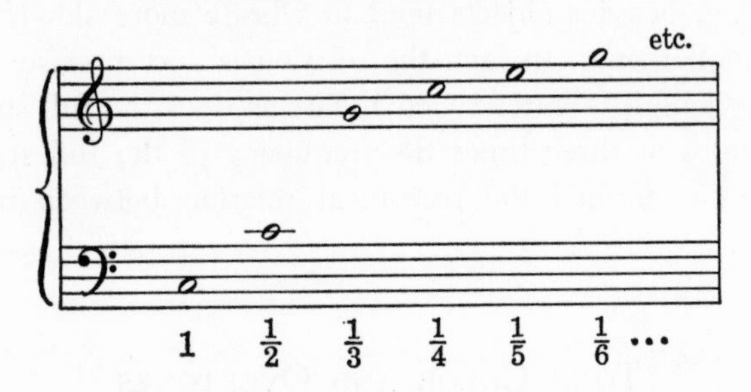

The overtones are usually so faint that we do not hear them as independent sounds; they contribute to the character of the fundamental tone. The overtone series as shown above is somewhat idealized. In practice each musical instrument tends to reinforce some overtones and to suppress others, due to such factors as the shape of the vibrating body, its method of being sounded, and the material of which it is made. The formation of nodes in a string is eliminated at the point where the string is plucked or sounded, which contributes to the character of the string tone. The particular shape of the bore of the clarinet suppresses the even-numbered overtones, and similar distortions of vibration are to be found in all instruments. In fact, the tone color of all musical instruments is in large part due to the characteristic ways in which each breaks up the impulse to vibrate into complex forms. Each instrument's beauty of sound is the result of its resistance as matter to the impulse toward simple vibration.

THE MUSICAL INSTRUMENTS

The vibrating materials of musical instruments may be strings, air, wood, metal or stretched membranes. In all of these, the same principles may be demonstrated. They vibrate because they are elastic, and they all exhibit node-and-loop formations. The body of air enclosed in a pipe, for example, is elastic: it undergoes waves of compression and rarefaction, while the general atmospheric pressure tends to restore it to a normal density. A smaller body of air vibrates more rapidly than a larger one. The vibrating air contained in a pipe such as the flute may be diminished by opening a hole in the side of the flute; then only the air from the mouthpiece to the opened hole vibrates as a unit and the pitch of the tone is raised because a smaller body of air has been set in motion. Before the hole is opened, the entire body of air in the flute vibrates as a unit.

The overtone series is not only of vital importance to the timbre of instruments, but plays a basic part in the technique of performing on wind instruments, through what is called *overblowing*. Beyond a certain point, an increase in the force of blowing does not produce a louder tone; instead, the pitch of the instrument jumps to one of the higher overtones. Once the player is in this higher register, he can, by means of the same finger technique which produced the scale above the fundamental tone, now produce a scale in a higher register, which extends enormously the range and versatility of these instruments.

The relative disuse of instruments of stone or metal, or of electrical devices, or of mechanical instruments such as music boxes, is due to their lack of an organic character. The instruments most widely used are those that closely suggest a living organism. Everyone, by virtue of the use of his lungs, and by the tensing of his muscles, feels an instinctive kinship with contained air and stretched string. The music which we feel speaks most closely to us is that activated most directly by an organism. The most beautiful tones are those which recall the qualities of the human voice, and the more the action of an instrument is mediated by a mechanism, the more tiring it becomes.

THE TRANSMISSION AND RECEPTION OF SOUND

A medium is needed to transmit vibrations from the generating object to the ear, otherwise no sounds could be heard. This is shown by the experiment of placing a ringing bell inside an airtight container, and then pumping the air out of it; as the air thins out, the sound of the bell becomes weaker until it can no longer be heard. When air is gradually returned to the container, the sound of the bell returns, and grows to its accustomed volume. Air, of course, is not the only medium for conducting sound—solids and liquids serve as well. In certain kinds of deafness the conduction of sound by the bones of the head may serve to by-pass the defective parts of the ear.

Singers, who produce sound inside the chest and throat, and violinists, who hold the instrument against the jaw, probably never hear the sounds they produce in exactly the same way as do listeners because their bodies serve to conduct vibrations as do their ears.

THE HUMAN EAR

Vibrations of the air are transmitted to the eardrum, which is connected to three bones, or ossicles: the *hammer*, the *anvil*, and the *stirrup*. The *footplate* of the stirrup transforms the mechanical vibrations into hydraulic vibrations in the canals, whence they are transmitted to the *organ of Corti*, a complex and minute organ whose functions are not well understood. It is believed that the organ of Corti breaks down complex vibrations into their simple components, and in some way reassembles and reinterprets them. It is from the organ of Corti that the auditory nerve carries electrical impulses to the brain; it is not clear how this organ transforms the hydraulic movements into electrical impulses; the process is possibly chemical. The ear is not a simple carrier of sounds to the brain from the surrounding air. We are accustomed to think of sound as being in the air about us, but it is more accurate to say that there is only vibration in the air. Sound is formed somewhere between ear and brain. Certainly the ear reinterprets vibration in a highly complex way, and is able to pick out sounds to which the attention is directed, while suppressing those not listened for, and is remarkably well able to distinguish the directions from which the sounds originate. The role of the ear can be traced in other ways; some of the sounds we "hear" as coming from musical instruments are never recorded by laboratory devices, and it is believed that they are formed inside the ear.

It is also important to note that the organs of balance, the semicircular canals, are located in the inner ear, and it is just possible that the sense of balance, or equilibrium, plays a major part in the aesthetic basis of music. One may even imagine that a work of musical art embodies an equilibrium of the impulses set forth in the music and that this connection is more than one of metaphor. We have observed already that the experience of gravity plays a fundamental part in organizing our concept of tonal space. The sense of balance, rooted as it is in the ear, is no less basic to our feeling for musical proportions and movements.

Gravity and balance, both among the most primitive sensations of our organism, centralize our experience of music as much as they do that of the physical world.

The acoustical foundations of music, then, rest upon these factors: (1) *Regularity of vibration;* since regular vibrations may be expressed in numerical terms, music, the art which expresses *measurement* and *proportion,* is possible. This is the distinctive character of music. The frequency range is a kind of space; the matter we find in that space is the measurements and proportions which the musician takes as his material. (2) *Complexity of vibration,* which clothes these proportions in sounds having a variety of distinctive tone colors, or timbres. (3) *Gravity and equilibrium.* We have observed that our experience of the frequency range as a tonal space moving from low to high is rooted in the increasing tension and brightness of high tones, which suggest a movement against gravity—elevation in space. Related to this, the sense of balance, based as it is in the ear, has bearing on our feeling for the impulses set forth by specific musical movements, where they may be expected to move, and how expected to resolve and finish.

CHAPTER 3

The Intellectual Foundations of Music

We have observed that music is the art which expresses measurement and proportion; this is its distinctive character. We may wish to see how this is so.

The Monochord

The monochord is the device which, since ancient times, has served for investigating and demonstrating the basic facts of music theory. It is simply a string of fixed length stretched over a sounding box, with a movable bridge. Modern forms of the instrument have more than one string, for convenience in sounding scales and harmonies. It is then not quite appropriate to call it a *monochord;* instead the term *sonometer* is used.

PROCEDURE

A string of any length may be taken as the starting point. Its value is given as unity, the number 1. A tone of differing pitch is produced by a different string length. If the original length is divided, the second tone is of higher pitch. If it is multiplied, the tone will be lower.

Such experiments may be ordered systematically according to the ratios of the string lengths used. The first string length is always 1.

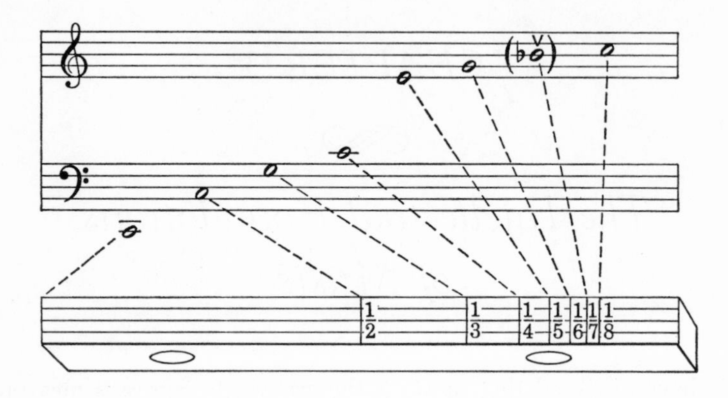

Each tone is related to the generator by virtue of the ratio of its string length to the string length of the generator.

The relation that each tone enters into with the generator is both spatial and numerical; the spatial relation is the musical interval and the numerical relation is the ratio of string lengths. The tones of the scale are not the materials of music; it is the intervals that each tone makes with the generator that comprise the materials of music. These intervals are clear and unmistakable shapes of musical space, being clear and definite no matter what pitches are used to sound them. They are what might be called sounding ratios.

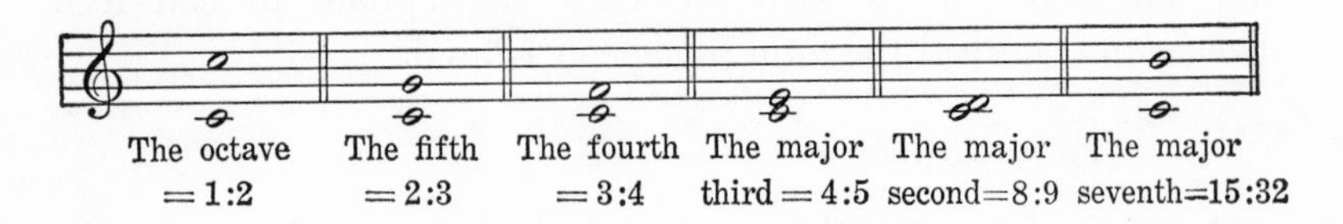

The octave = 1:2 The fifth = 2:3 The fourth = 3:4 The major third = 4:5 The major second = 8:9 The major seventh = 15:32

Number is today regarded as a somewhat shadowy abstraction but was seen rather differently in the era in which our musical system originated. The entire world was held to be well ordered and built on number; its astronomical cycles as well as the cycles of life were based on numerical foundations. The idea of the universal harmony ruling not only the universe, but also the social order and the life of the individual as well, is a very old one and music was considered to be only one narrow sphere in which the divine harmony could be demonstrated. Whatever the status of such thinking today, our musical scale had its origin in such considerations.

THE BASIC MUSICAL NUMBERS

Our music is based on the numbers 1 through 5 and on the ratios into which each is brought with the others; or, more accurately, only on the *prime* numbers up to five: 1, 2, 3, and 5.* Our music excludes all tones corresponding to all prime numbers after 5: 7, 11, 13, 17, 19, and so on. The tones corresponding to these numbers cannot be sounded on a keyboard, they have no names, and even cannot be shown in our notation except by approximations.

THE SOUND-QUALITIES OF THE MUSICAL NUMBERS

One. To the number 1 corresponds the length of string selected as the starting point. It may be of any length and the corresponding tone may be of any pitch. The same relations will apply no matter what tone is sounded. For simplicity in the use of our musical notation we may use the tone C. The tone by itself is in no relation to anything and therefore has no definite character other than that of having a definite pitch, a fixed place in tonal space.

Two. Dividing the string by two produces our first interval, which is called in our musical system the *octave.*

* A prime nunber is any number which cannot be divided evenly by a smaller number (except of course 1); 9 is not a prime number, as it may be divided by 3; 11 is a prime, as there is no other number except 1 which can divide it evenly; 15 is not a prime, but 17 and 19 are.

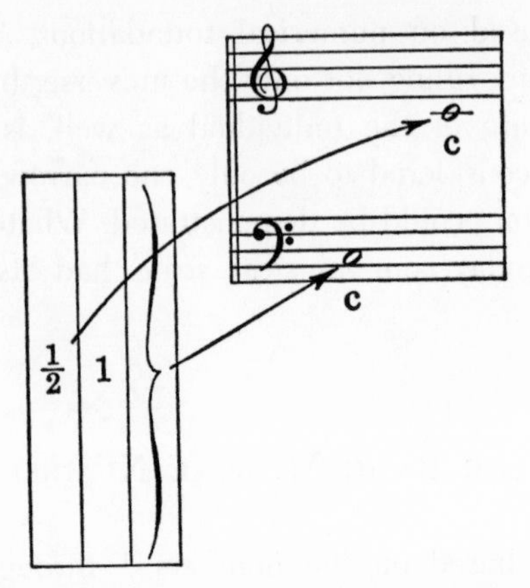

The two tones blend into one sound, so perfectly that they both are given the same name, C, one low, the other high. In some way they express an identity—the *same* tone projected to a higher or lower point. Men of all ages and nations agree that tones in this ratio are identical in some sense, they merge into one. When men and women sing together, they usually sing an octave apart, but no one doubts that they are singing together. This is not the case for any other type of interval; all other intervals are combinations of different tones, not identical ones.

This identity of octave tones has a fundamental implication for music. It tells us first of all that any tone, corresponding to any number whatever, recurs over and over again in musical space. We have not yet investigated the other numbers, such as 3 or 5, but whatever tones they may produce in relation to the fundamental tone, they too can be repeated at different octaves. Whatever tone

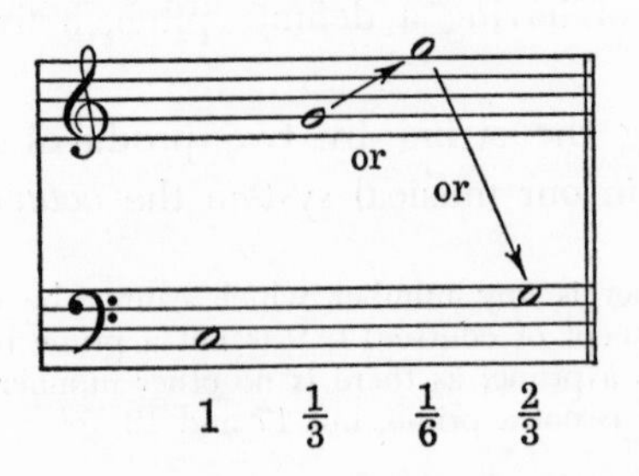

corresponds to the ratio 1/3 can recur at a higher or lower octave simply by dividing or multiplying by two: the tones 2/3, 1/6, 1/12, are all higher or lower octaves of the original value, 1/3.

We see also that any number may be divided or multiplied repeatedly by two without changing its musical character; we are simply shifting the tone up or down by octaves.

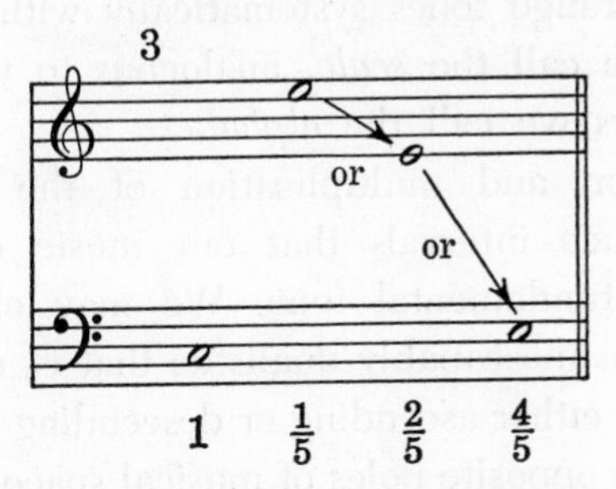

And finally we see that the interval we call the octave is unique among the intervals in that it is a space into which all other tonal values may be projected. Any tone too high or too low may be transposed without loss of identity until it finds itself within the octave selected.

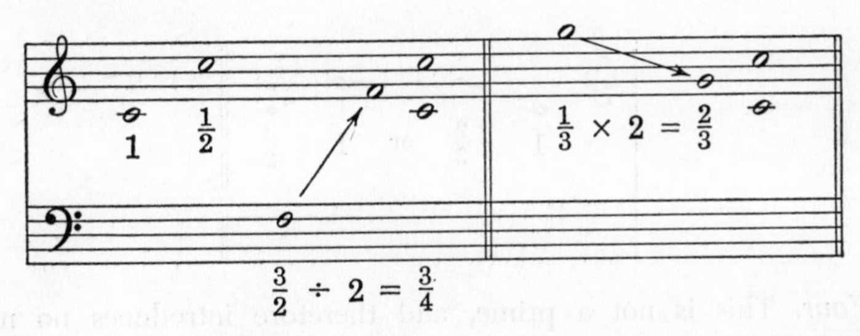

Hitherto we have been confronted with a tonal space of enormous extent, from the lowest limit of audibility up to the highest, and with an infinity of possible tones to fill it. Now we see that the space framed by the octave contains all values and serves, so to speak, as a microcosm.

The Greeks expressed their awareness of this by their names for the various intervals; what we call the fifth, they called *diapente,* "through five tones"; the fourth they called *diatessaron,* "through four tones," and so on; but they called the octave *diapason,* "through *all* tones." Our term, octave, is a later one, from the Latin, and tells us merely that we fill the octave with eight steps, but ignores the unique character of this interval.

That the octave is a kind of microcosm for all possible tones enables us to arrange tones systematically within the octave and achieve what we call the *scale,* analogous to that systematic arranging of letters we call the *alphabet.*

Three. Division and multiplication of the string length by three will produce intervals that our music calls fifths, above and below the fundamental tone. We may observe that every musical relation is inescapably dualistic; that is, every interval may be constructed in either ascending or descending direction. The two directions are the opposite poles of musical space.

The interval of the fifth, generated by multiplying or dividing by three, is the strongest possible harmony between two different tones. It possesses a certain ambiguity of character, as with any two tones taken by themselves: it is not possible to tell which is the generator and whether the construction is ascending or descending:

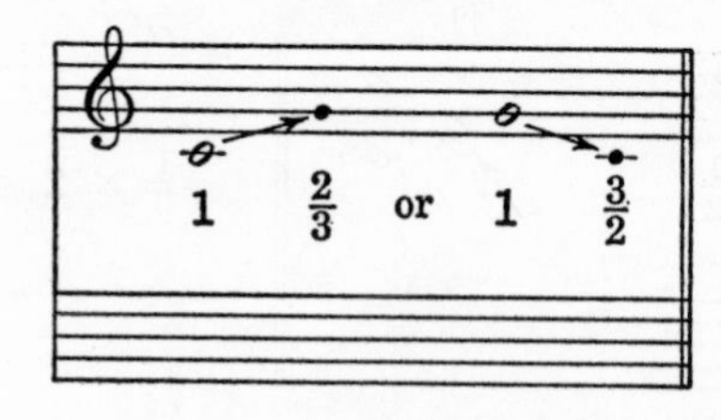

Four. This is not a prime, and therefore introduces no new interval. It is simply another octave of two (see example on page 23).

Five. The next prime number, 5, produces tone E, a major third above, or A-flat, a major third below the central tone. The number 5 makes clear that which has been heretofore indeterminate, the mode of construction of the fifth, ascending or descending; in the fifth, C—G, we cannot tell which tone is the fundamental, but the addition of a third will tell us. If the lower tone, C, is the generator, the addition of E confirms this to the ear. Conversely, if the upper tone, G, is the generator, the fifth will be filled by E-flat, the major third below the generator.

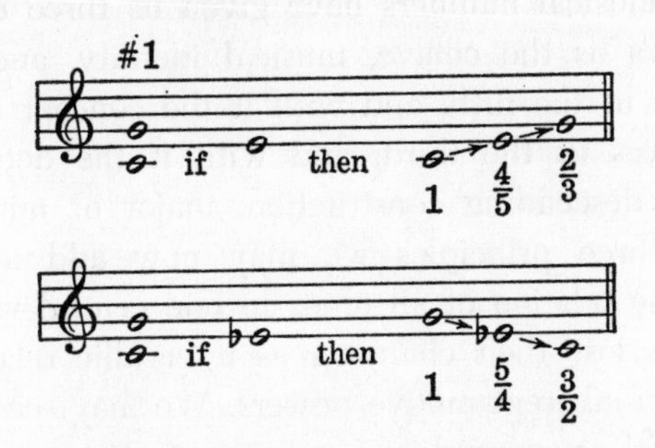

The prime number 5, then, determines the direction, ascending or descending, in which intervals and harmonies are built. The ascending direction is generally referred to in terms of major scales and major harmonies, the descending in terms of minor scales and harmonies.

We have observed that the ascending tones according to the number series occur as a natural phenomenon in the overtone series. There is no phenomenon in nature corresponding to the descending order of tones below the fundamental. The natural overtone series gives us an inescapable feeling for regarding the lowest sounding tone as the foundation of the tones above it, a feeling which we carry even into descending relationships. Thus, in the minor triad, as shown below, although the tones are numerically derived from the generator above, our practical music derives all relations from the lowest sounding tone upwards, and although the generators are E and C, respectively, we refer to them as A minor and F minor triads, thinking of them from the lowest tone upwards.

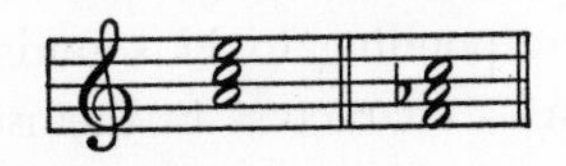

The minor mode—relations built in descending direction—has often been misread as merely a modification of the major system, but in reality is a coherent system in itself, though less favored by acoustical facts.

The basic musical numbers have given us three different principles: 2 gives us the octave, musical identity, and with it the scale; 3 gives us the fifth, and with it the concept of polarity or motion; 5 gives us the third, and with it the determination of ascending or descending construction, major or minor.

To these three principles we may now add a fourth, that of *tonality,* the relation of all tones to one central value. Without tonality, tones lose their character as intervallic relationships and music loses its inherent motive powers. We may see that the idea of the interval is an ambiguous concept. It may mean simply two tones sounded together or in succession, it may mean the ratio of the two tones, it may mean the space framed by the tones, or, finally, the number of steps with which that space is filled. Thus without the concept of tonality—the relation of tones to a central value—their intervallic relationships of identity, polarity, or modality disappear, and they become mere tones, with no specific character and quality.

We have remarked that our music is based only on the prime numbers 2, 3, and 5 and their combinations, and that all other prime numbers are excluded. It might be thought, without further investigation, that a music based upon so few values might be rather impoverished, and that a music which embraced more numerical values would have greater variety and richness. But, though this may seem paradoxical, it is actually the other way around. The intervals corresponding to the basic numbers are clear and definite in character, while the tones corresponding to other numbers are more and more crowded together in space until finally it becomes difficult to tell them apart. The tone corresponding to 7 sounds (in ascending direction) like a B-flat, but out of tune; that corresponding to 11 sounds like a bad F-sharp. We do not hear them as characters in themselves but as approximations of the simpler values. It is not merely a matter of habit that we are used to certain intervals and not to others, but rather that only certain intervals are inherent in our grasp of experience. We can see this with respect to vision as well as hearing. Anyone looking at a tripod sees immediately that he is looking at an object with three basic parts. If he looks at a long shelf laden with books he knows only that he sees many books; just how many is something that cannot be directly seen, but must be determined by counting, which is an entirely different process. Once they are counted, he knows—though he still does not see—the number of books. If he has miscounted, his sight does not correct him.

More simply, the basic numbers can be grasped by the senses, hearing as well as sight, not only by their simplicity but by their distinctive characters as well. These are so much a part of our perceptions that we accept as satisfactory even a crude approximation to these basic ratios. The ability of the mind and the senses to accept approximations to values for the values themselves is not a matter of imprecision; it is what makes intelligible experiences possible. Musical instruments almost never sound musical ratios with great accuracy. Changes in temperature and humidity are constantly forcing them out of tune. In fact, some instruments are kept deliberately "out of tune"; this is what the musician means by "the well tempered keyboard"—an instrument kept systematically out of tune. Certain inaccuracies are, for technical reasons, inherent in all musical relationships; the well tempered system distributes these inaccuracies evenly over all the steps of the scale. Nevertheless we accept the slightly false intervals of the piano or organ for the true ones, because the mind is able to recognize certain numerical values. It is these values which are the intellectual foundations of music.

CHAPTER 4

The Scale

Most people begin their practical work in music by learning to sing the scale, usually to the well known syllables "do-re-mi-fa-sol-la-ti-do." This is the simplest and most natural way to begin. But though the scale in this form serves quite properly as our musical ABC, we should not think of it as a real beginning, as though it were an element of nature. It is an artifact, the product of theoretical and practical work over many centuries.

The scale is a product of the basic numbers and ratios and the result of their corresponding intervals being projected into the space of one octave. These are:

ascending:	1/2	2/3	3/4	4/5	5/6
	octave	fifth	fourth	major third	minor third
descending:	2/1	3/2	4/3	5/4	6/5

ascending:	8/9	9/10	15/16
	major whole step*	minor whole step	half step
descending:	9/8	10/9	16/15

These intervals can be projected into the octave in several ways, and accordingly the scale can assume several forms, depending on whether this is done in ascending or descending order, or in a balance of the two.

* The difference between the two whole steps 8/9, and 9/10 is very slight, and in practice they are taken as identical. But in theory D is slightly closer to E than C is to D, when C is the generator.

If the fifth is projected into the octave both ascending and descending, we are given the chief points of the scale, which everyone learns in elementary harmony under the names tonic, subdominant, and dominant.

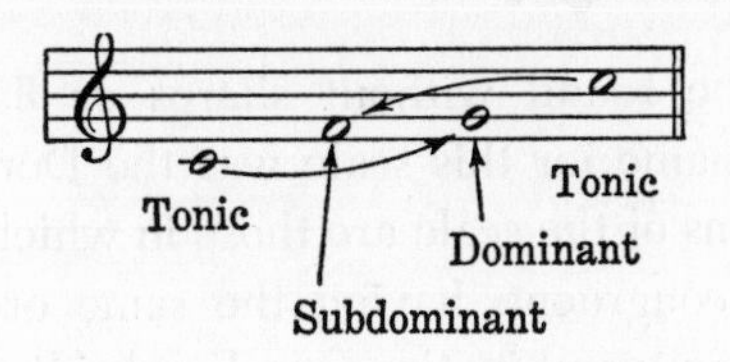

As we have seen, there are three kinds of steps with which to fill the gaps in the scale, the major whole step, the minor whole step, and the half step.

If the gaps are filled ascending, the result is our familiar C major scale.

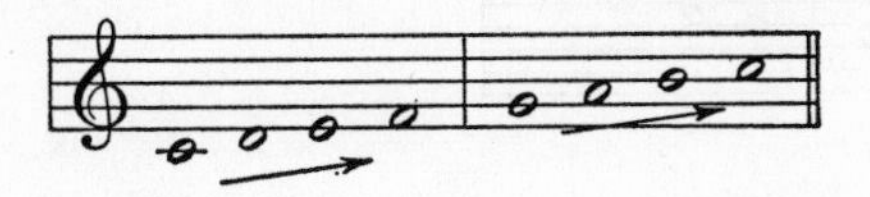

We may note that the scale consists of two identical parts, the tones C through F having the same order of steps as G through C. The term for each group of four steps is *tetrachord,* and we see that the two tetrachords are congruent. If the same sequence of steps (major whole step, minor whole step, and half step) is arraged in descending order, then the scale takes the following form:

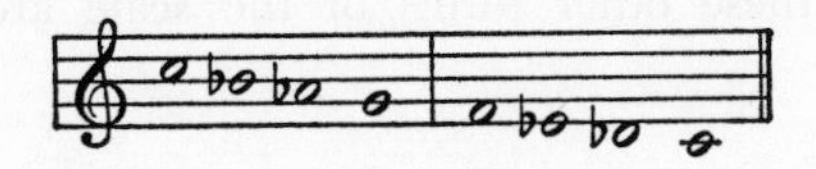

We find this same scale without flat signs in the octave starting from E. This scale was called by medieval theorists the Phrygian mode.

And, again, if the chief points of the scale are linked by an equal balance of steps ascending and descending, the scale assumes the following shape:

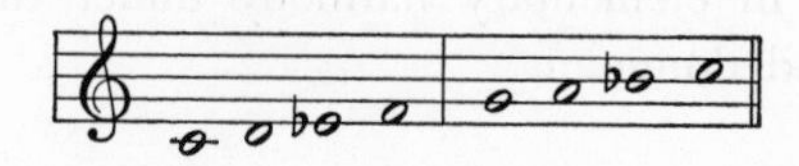

This form may be found without sharps or flats in the octave on D. The older name for this scale was the Dorian mode.

These three forms of the scale are those in which both tetrachords of the scale are congruent, having the same order of steps.

There are other combinations and subsidiary forms of the scale.

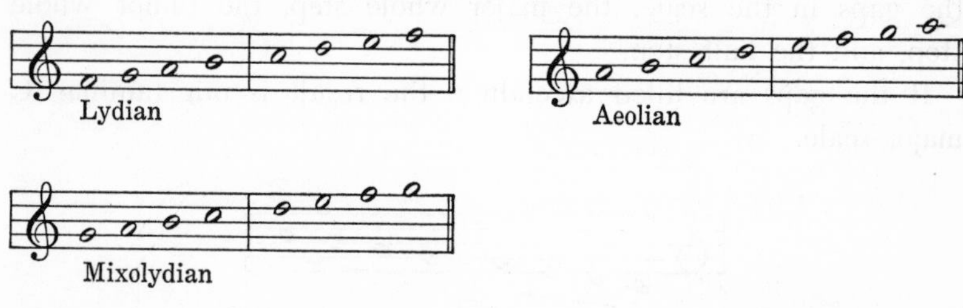
Lydian

Aeolian

Mixolydian

The names Dorian, Phrygian, and so on, were assigned the various scales by medieval theorists who named them after the Greek tribes in whose music they were thought to have predominated. Later researches have demonstrated that the names were confused, but custom and usage have preserved them. By the eighteenth century this modal system was eclipsed by our familiar major-minor system, though never completely. Beethoven and Brahms, among others, essayed compositions using modal material. In our own time these other forms of the scale are again coming to the fore.

KEYS AND ACCIDENTALS

The scale in any of its forms may be built on any desired tone. Thus, the major scale may be built on G as well as on C. In order to preserve the proper order of half steps in relation to whole steps, in the tetrachord D—G, the tone F has to be raised a half step to F-sharp. Transposition of the scale to D requires a second sharp.

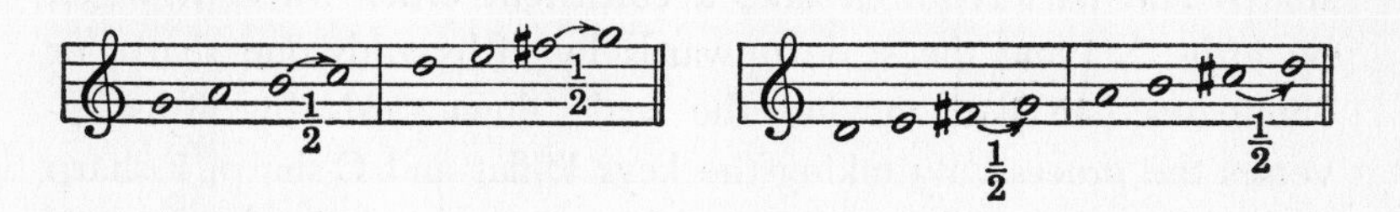

Again, transposition of the scale from C to F necessitates lowering B to B-flat. In a similar manner, the scale may be transposed to any other tone, by the progressive chromatic alteration of the tones of the scale.

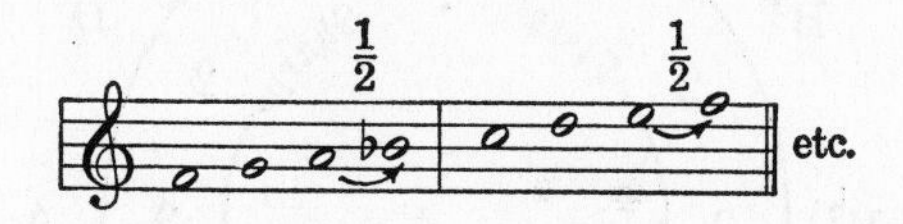

The chromatic alteration of the seven main tones results in a total set of twenty-one different tones.

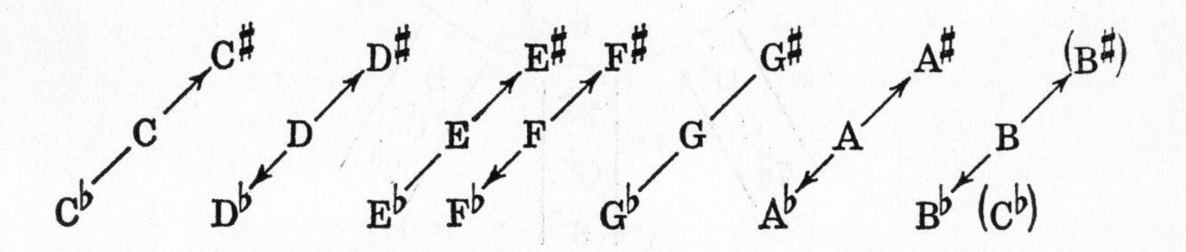

But the tones C-sharp and D-flat, D-sharp and E-flat, E and F-flat, E-sharp and F, G-sharp and A-flat, etc., are so close to one another that in practice they are taken as identical. They are called enharmonically equivalent; the term means sounding as one. The same key on the piano serves for C-sharp as well as for D-flat, and they are distinguished according to their notation; C-sharp means C raised, moving toward D; D-flat means D lowered, moving toward C.

THE CIRCLE OF FIFTHS

The successive transpositions of the scale and the successive sharps and flats required take a consistent order when arranged by fifths. Moving the scale upwards by fifths adds one sharp, or eliminates one flat; moving the scale downwards by fifths reverses the process. By taking the keys D-flat and C-sharp, F-sharp and G-flat, and C-flat and B as the same, the series becomes a circle which returns to its starting point.

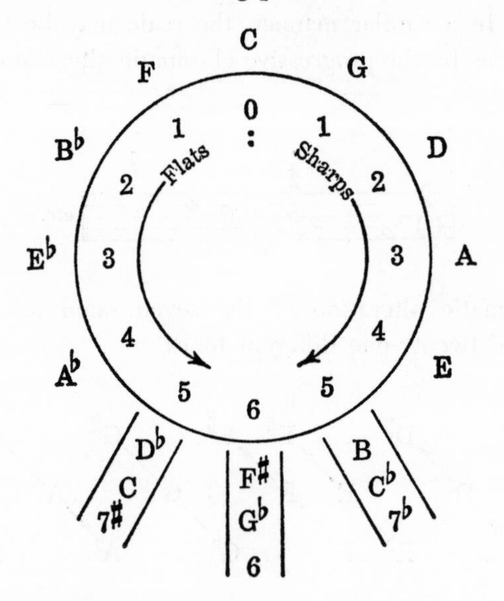

KEYS, MODES, AND SCALES

The terms C major, G minor, and so on, tell us two things: the particular octave within which the scale is built and which particular form of the scale—ascending, descending, and so forth—has been adopted. The key tells us, then, which tone is the tonic. The term *mode* is simply the scholastic term for a particular form of the scale, Lydian, Phrygian, and so on. The scale is the result of the basic numbers of our system.

Our scale is called the *diatonic* scale; a scale that uses two kinds of steps, whole steps (for example C to D) and half steps (B to C and E to F). (In practice, the distinction between the major and minor whole steps, that is 8/9 and 9/10, is ignored.) There is no scale resulting from the use of more prime numbers than ours, or at least none such has yet been devised. But there is a scale which uses fewer prime numbers. If we eliminate from our scale those tones and intervals derived from the number 5, limiting it to the primes through 3, the result is the pentatonic scale, without half steps.

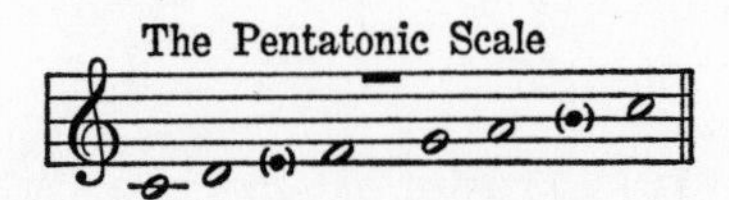
The Pentatonic Scale

Each form of the scale represents a way of moving to and from the tonic. Melodies might be thought to move through the various points of the scale. But there is also another form of progression, that from one form of the scale to another and from one central tone to another. A composition may begin and end in A minor, though during its course there may occur a metamorphosis into C major. For a time, the piece moves about another central tone, and in a different manner, before resuming its original form. Such changes, which are called *modulations,* represent only more extended and varied developments of the movement about the original tonal center.

Part Two

THE SUBSTANCE OF MUSIC

CHAPTER 5

Melody

Melody is perhaps the most puzzling feature of music. Music theory has much to say on a variety of subjects—harmony, counterpoint, rhythm and meter, form and analysis, and orchestration—but on the subject of melody offers nothing at all comparable to the centuries-old theory of harmony, replete as it is with definitions, rules, and pedagogical devices for leading the student through its details step by step. Harmony might be termed the discipline which explores the simultaneous combinations of tones. There is no similar discipline for telling us how they may be joined in succession. This is left to the artist.

The mystery concerning melody stems from its very nature: it represents music in its most concrete and individualized form. The rhythm and the harmony that belong to a particular melody are fairly general features. The rhythm can be represented by tones different from those in the melody, or even without tones at all; the harmony can be found in other compositions and has more than one way of being materialized. A melody is just its own unique combination of tones and rhythms. Melody—unlike harmony and rhythm, which it shares with other compositions—is that which gives the composition its individual shape. Its invention is as much an aesthetic process as it is a technical one; it is not so much invented as discovered. To be sure, it is quite possible to abstract from a melody, by eliminating repeated tones, passing tones, embellishments, and so on, the skeleton of the melody—those tones which are the principal points of its progression.

But this is a secondary act, of analysis and dissection, and the melody belongs to that which came before the dissection. It is this difficulty which has left music theorists so much at a loss for some generally valid study of melody. Nevertheless, some description is possible.

A melody is, first, a succession of tones of differing pitch. Generally, stepwise motion balances motion by leaps, and ascending and descending motion balance one another. The restoration of balance is frequently delayed or not immediately apparent.

A melody outlines an ordered progression.

It displays an over-all balance between ascending or descending motion.

Leaps in a melody generally are filled in immediately after the leap occurs.

A melody may directly unfold harmonies or successions of harmonies or may attempt to be as free as possible of chordal traits.

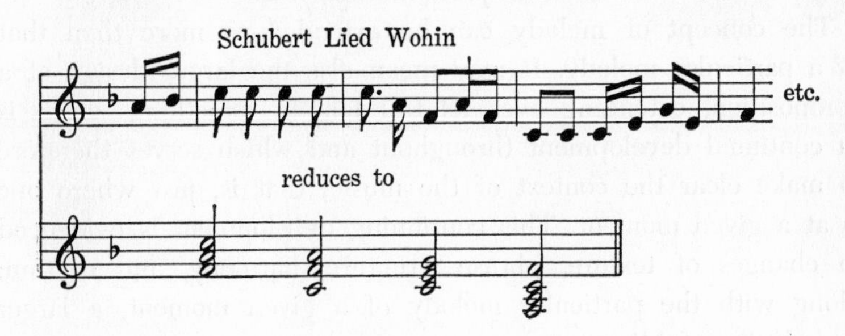

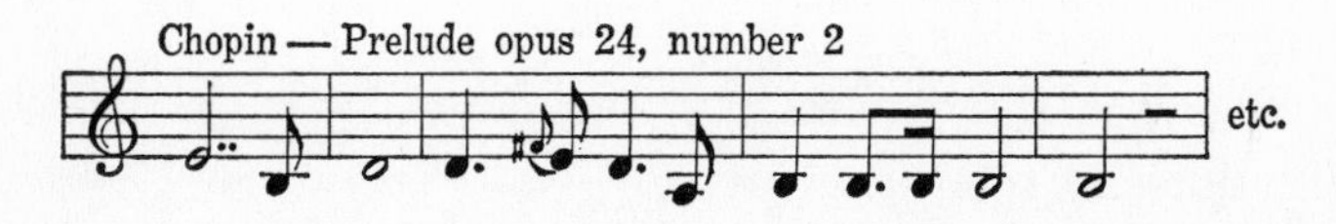

The most fundamental feature of melody is continuity. A melody is something produced by one continuing source, by one flow of energy, even when is it silent, even when its motives are disassembled and tossed back and forth between different instruments of the orchestra. It is a shape not deducible from its components alone; we recognize its shape in a manner analogous to our recognition of an object or a person in a picture consisting of discontinuous dots of light and dark. In the same way, the melody is a continuity though its component notes are discontinuous.

Here the concept of melody is joined with considerations of rhythm and meter. Motives and phrase units have rhythmic features as essential as the melodic intervals and progressions. The smallest coherent musical unit, the motive, represents the fusion of two elements, change of pitch and rhythm, into one unit.

Stepwise progression, whether it is immediate or delayed by leaps, is the basis of melody, and consequently the real foundation of melodic motion is the scale. Consistency is given to melody by its stepwise movement, variety by its leaps. Without any leaps, the melody may appear as an aimless wandering up and down the notes of the scale. Where leaps predominate, the melody may fall into a series of disjointed fragments.

The concept of melody can be extended to more than that of a particular melody. It may mean also the larger design of a composition, extending over its full length, something which is in continual development throughout and which serves therefore to make clear the context of the music, that is, just where one is at a given moment. This continuing development is evidenced in changes of texture, phrase structure, harmony, and rhythm; along with the particular melody of a given moment, a larger melody is unfolding.

CHAPTER 6

Harmony and Polyphony

Harmony and polyphony are the two features unique in Western music. The entire history of this music could be written as the history of harmonic and polyphonic developments.

HARMONY

The term *harmony* was originally not even a musical term. For the Greeks it meant joining or fitting together, as in carpentry work. Its musical meaning for the Greeks was the joining together of the successive tones of a melody. Today it has a number of meanings. Primarily, harmony means the joining together of different tones in simultaneous combinations. The term is also applied to the individual combinations; each is called "a harmony" or "a chord." Finally, it means that branch of music theory which studies the laws of harmony: how particular harmonies are constructed, their character and function, and their syntax—how harmonies may succeed one another in a logical and coherent manner.

THE FOUNDATIONS OF HARMONY

The same numbers which create the scale are the foundations for harmony. The tones corresponding to the first six numbers are:

This is harmony in its strongest form, the order in which tones join most perfectly. We note that this harmony is composed of only three different tones, two being repeated. By eliminating the repeated tones, we have harmony in its simplest form—the *triad.* The simplest vocabulary of harmony is gained by building triads on each step of the scale, by consideration of their properties and their possible order of succession.

The strongest and most natural progression from one harmony to another is that along the circle of fifths. We may recall that the interval of the fifth affords the strongest possible harmony between two different tones. Harmonic progression along this path is the most natural, and a succession of harmonies not in this relation has the character of a delay or suspension of this natural progression.

HARMONY AND THE SCALE

The scale gives shape and moving force to harmonic progressions. Certain points of the scale have a special dynamic significance. In the C major scale, the tone C is the generator of the scale and its center of gravity—hence its name, the *tonic*. Musical motion begins and ends with the tonic; the other tones literally gravitate about this center. The tones F and G represent the principal points of the scale, other than the tonic; they are termed, respectively, the *subdominant* and the *dominant*.

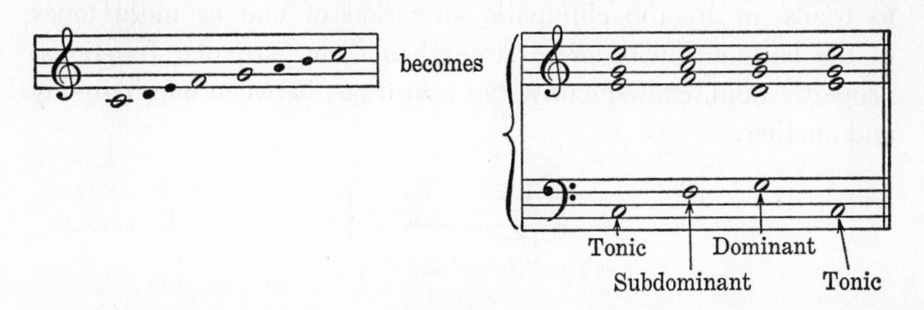

This arrangement is the ground plan of all harmonic progressions; it is the moving force that harmony provides music and the field upon which melodic and polyphonic developments unfold. There are, to be sure, many other possible harmonic progressions which are found in music; these have the character of delaying or expanding the basic progression, or of presenting it in a veiled or altered form.

FUNCTIONAL DISSONANCE

The vocabulary of harmony is enriched by adding to triads dissonant tones which serve to increase their dynamic properties. Thus, the dominant appears frequently with the addition of a tone a seventh above its root; whence its name, *dominant seventh chord.*

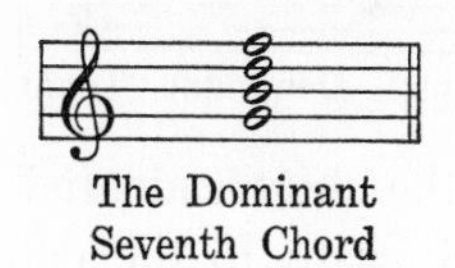

The Dominant Seventh Chord

The subdominant harmony is frequently reinforced by a sixth added to the triad.

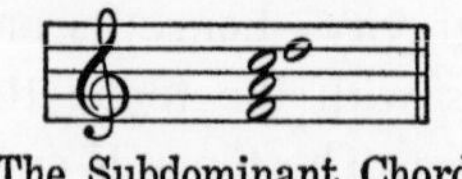

The Subdominant Chord
with added Sixth

A large vocabulary of harmonies is created by the addition of tones to triads, or by the chromatic alteration of one or more tones of the harmony in order to strengthen their particular functional properties and, consequently, the transitions between one harmony and another.

The "Neapolitan Sixth"
Chord
a Chromatic Alteration of
the Subdominant

SECONDARY HARMONIES

The simple cadential progression (see example, page 43) may be enriched and expanded by the interpolation of other harmonies, called secondary,* and their related functions. A given point in the progression may be expanded by treating it, temporarily, as though it were a tonic.

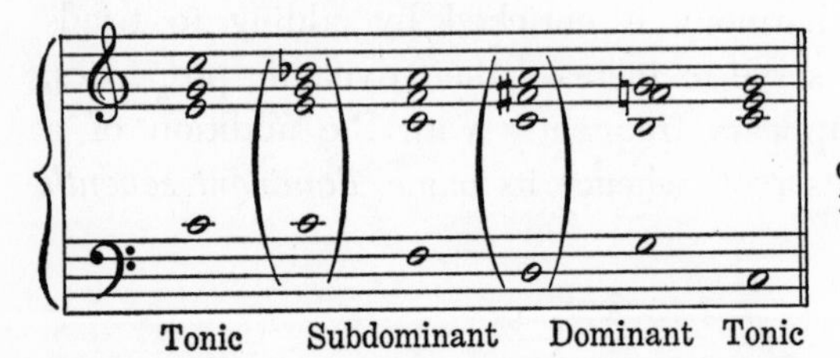

The bracketed chords are dominants of the harmonies immediately following them

This process led from the short cadential sentences of such composers as Corelli and Scarlatti to the enormous structures of the classic composers, Haydn, Mozart, and Beethoven.

* Primary harmonies are simply those of the scale itself. Secondary harmonies are those foreign to the scale but explicable by reference to one or another primary harmony.

MODULATION

The *sonata* of the classical period is that music in which the moving power of harmony is the first consideration. As this power served to create larger and larger structures, a new development appeared, that of the polarity and conflict of two opposing tonalities. A sonata beginning in a certain key may appear to have shifted, after a time, to another key, another center of gravity. The shift from one tonal center to another is termed *modulation*, and plays a large part in the constructive power of harmony.

Modulation is based on ambiguities of sound and therefore of function. The traid C-E-G may be at once the subdominant of G and the tonic of C. A shift in its character—that is, of its treatment—will indicate a shift of tonality. Other harmonies, when chromatically altered, may become completely ambiguous; belonging to any of several possible keys, they serve as links between them.

The conflict of two tonalities and the forces which each exerts play a major part in the events of the sonata.

CONSONANCE AND DISSONANCE

A dissonant harmony is one expressing movement and energy. A consonant harmony is one which is static and expresses the disappearance or receding of energy.

The concept of dissonance rests upon that of a tonal center, a tone, or group of tones, against which all others are measured. A tone by itself is neither consonant nor dissonant; it is meaningless. The same is true for an interval. If we sound what is called in elementary theory a dissonant interval, say, D against C, it is impossible to say which tone is the dissonant one, without some background or context to tell us which is the tonal center. If we think of it against a background of B-flat, then C is the dissonant tone, but if the background is C, then D is the dissonant tone and the resolution, the relaxation of dissonance to consonance, moves accordingly.

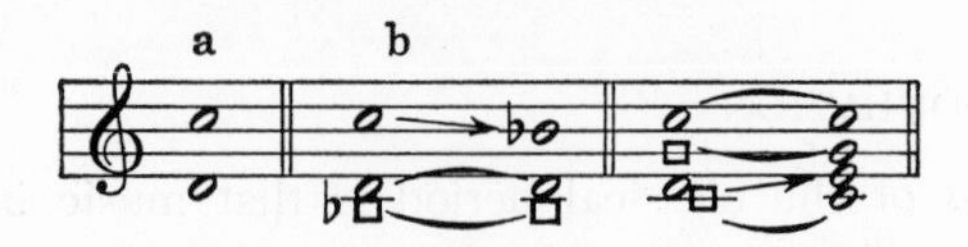

If we have no background in mind, the interval becomes static and harmonically indifferent. And even the intervals of elementary theory which are called consonant may be given a dissonant meaning by a suitable background.

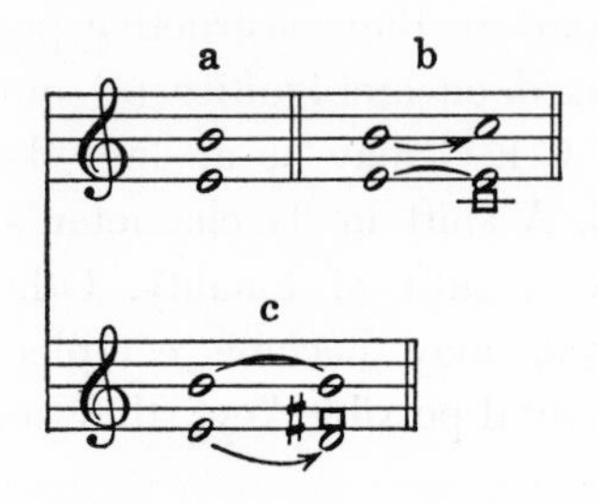

The same may be said for triads and for more complex harmonies. Almost any of these may be either consonant or dissonant, given a suitable context. The triad G-B-D is by itself consonant and therefore static. In a context of C major it acquires the function of the dominant and so becomes active, dissonant. Even a harmony which by itself is dissonant can become, for the duration of a measure or a phrase, the stable background upon which melodies unfold, until the inherent dynamism of the chord and the energy of its context move the harmony to a further progression.

Without the concept of tonality, the materials of music lose their inherent properties and become static. One recalls the saying of Heraclitus that the invisible harmony is mightier than the visible. In any event, without the invisible harmony, the visible harmony, the tones and intervals sounding at a given time, lose their expressive force and become characterless and for practical purposes interchangeable. Music without tonality then requires some special or artificial means of creating motion.

POLYPHONY

Polyphony is that music in which more than one melody unfolds at a given time. As a developed art, it is, like harmony, the unique achievement of Western music. The music of the East has developed melody and rhythm to high levels. Indeed, compared to some, the melodies and rhythms of the West appear rather stiff and limited. It was perhaps necessary for melody and rhythm to suffer a certain simplification during the apprenticeships of polyphony and harmony. The theory of harmony was developed in order to permit independent melodies to fit together in some coherent way. Without harmonic considerations, two melodies going on at once would represent a mere accident, as when a musician in the street adds a melody to one we are singing or playing. Harmony deals with those intervallic combinations which may be considered coherent.

The development of polyphony required more accurate notation of time and rhythm. As simultaneous melodies had to fit together, at least at crucial points, they had to reach such points of articulation at the same time, and a rhythmic notation was developed. This took centuries of work, and like any language, is still evolving today.

THE DEVELOPMENT OF HARMONY THROUGH POLYPHONY

With the practice of polyphony developed the theory of harmony, those intervals at which melodies join together. Early polyphony consisted of simultaneous soundings of a given melody at one or another interval. Later, in composed polyphony, the melodies of a composition were written successively. To the first melody, which was normally something preexistent—usually a segment of Gregorian chant—a second melody would be added, and then a third.

With the gradual development of three- and four-part writing, the theory of harmony evolved steadily toward the concept of the triad, a process that took several centuries. The masterworks of the Renaissance, from Dunstable to Josquin, and from Josquin to Lassus, are music unsurpassed by any subsequent achievements. But harmonic thinking is not foremost. At any given moment in these works, the harmony is merely a product of melodies going on at the same time. Harmonic considerations are in evidence only at special points, the cadences.

POLYPHONY AND THE CADENCE

Polyphony and harmony join at the cadences, where the melodies stop. It was at these points that harmonic progressions began to be taken as important in themselves. Between cadences the harmonies succeeded one another without much consideration of syntax. If the final of a composition is C, the simplest approach to the final is by step:

It was also common enough, in Renaissance music, to add a third voice, and a fourth, as follows:

The voices were at first simply fitted in at those points which were consonant, but it was noticed in time that not only the harmony of the final, but also that of the approach to the final formed a specific unit, the triad, and that the generator of the triad approaching, which we called the dominant, was a fifth above the generator of the tonic triad. The tonic harmony could also be approached simply by:

The generator of this harmony is also a fifth from the tonic, the fifth below. We call it the subdominant.

Both subdominant and dominant set up a gravitation to the tonic, though that of the dominant is somewhat stronger. The progressions were combined to set up the full cadence, creating the strongest gravitation to the tonic.

Another form of close was that used in the old Phrygian mode:

This could be employed as an approach to the dominant, so that the full cadence could appear in this form:

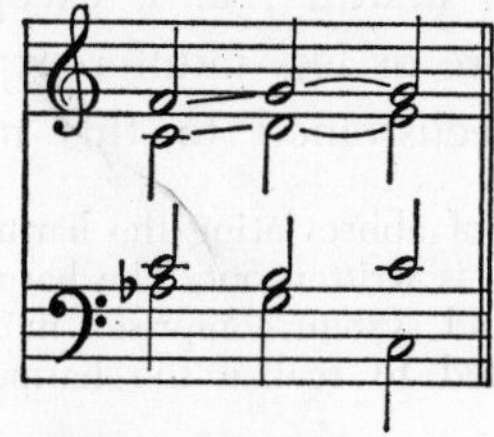

with the subdominant slightly altered.

Out of such considerations as these—fitting melodies together at cadences—grew the awareness of harmonies as specific units, and of the strength of specific progressions, as well as their application not only to the ends of phrases and sections, but to the entire unfolding of the music.

It took two centuries, from the works of Dunstable to the theoretical writings of Zarlino, for the concept of harmony as a thing in itself to be clearly formulated. Its evolution is marked by the statement of the theorist Pietro Aron at the beginning of the sixteenth century that composers were no longer writing the melodies of their polyphonic works successively, but were writing each part with all the others in mind. The concept of the triad was clarified only at the end of the sixteenth century.

It took two more centuries for composers to learn how to operate with the triad and with triadic progressions as autonomous entities. The further progress of harmonic thinking is marked, partly by the baroque system of figured bass,* which abbreviates triadic harmonies in a musical shorthand, and by the formulations of Rameau in the eighteenth century, who speaks of the tonic as the harmonic center (he is the first to do so) and who first formulated the idea that melodies are harmonies unfolded in time. The musical practice of the generation after Bach definitively established the cadential progression as the architectural principle of music. This progression reached its height in the classic masters, Haydn, Mozart, Beethoven, and Brahms. Their music stands at least in one respect at the opposite pole from that of the Renaissance masters, such as Josquin, Willaert, or Lassus. For the earlier composers, harmony is simply the result of polyphony, of adding one melody to another, and, except at cadential points in their music, it is more or less indifferent what harmony follows another. To ears unaccustomed to this music—and there is a

* Figured bass is a way of abbreviating the harmony. Only the bass part—the lowest sounding tones—is written out. The harmonies built upon this bass are indicated by a shorthand system comprised mostly of numbers. The keyboard performer is expected to realize the harmony from the abbreviated notation.

large public for which older music is a dead language only recently revived—the harmony has a curiously unnatural, suspended character. Familiar and expected progressions do not occur, simply because the harmony was not conceived as having specific properties of its own. In compositions of the classic period, on the other hand, polyphonic writing, no matter how skillful, is really bound by the harmonic progression and unfolds it. Melody and rhythm are subordinated to harmony, and shaped by it.

The romantic era brought with it much experimentation, both rhythmic and harmonic. It created music of increased color and richness of sound, but of diminished power of motion. Harmonies became expressive rather than dynamic during this period, and accordingly lost their power of creating large and extended structures. The increasing exploitation of harmonic ambiguity and the resultant clouding of tonality brought about the loss of a generally valid language of harmony. New and arbitrary combinations of tones were taken as consonant harmonies, as in the experiments of Debussy and Scriabin. Such combinations were the expressions of personal talents and personal experiments, rather than expressions of theoretical facts. By the twentieth century, harmonic thinking had become almost entirely experimental. Perhaps the only feature upon which musicians agreed was the avoidance of the old triadic harmony. Along with this experimentalism arose a renewed interest in polyphony. Melodic lines were written almost completely without regard to their harmonic clashes, the only consideration being possibly that of keeping the clashes as dissonant as possible.

The condition of harmony today is that the old triadic harmony and the classic concept of tonality have disappeared as structural principles; nothing has as yet come to the fore to replace them other than various personalities and their disciples. There exists today no theory of harmony which is the logical and coherent result of undeniable facts and consistent logic. The theory of harmony as is it taught today is merely historical, that is, it observes what particular musicians have done in the past but makes no attempts to establish itself on firm principles. Even the important insights and formulations of Hugo Riemann and Heinrich Schenker are retrospective, and have not directly created a new theory of harmony. The essence of any such theory will have to be a valid distinction between consonance and dissonance and a valid formulation of tonality. The older theory of harmony was based upon the outer regions of the senarius (4:5:6); a new harmony might be developed out of attention to the inner regions:

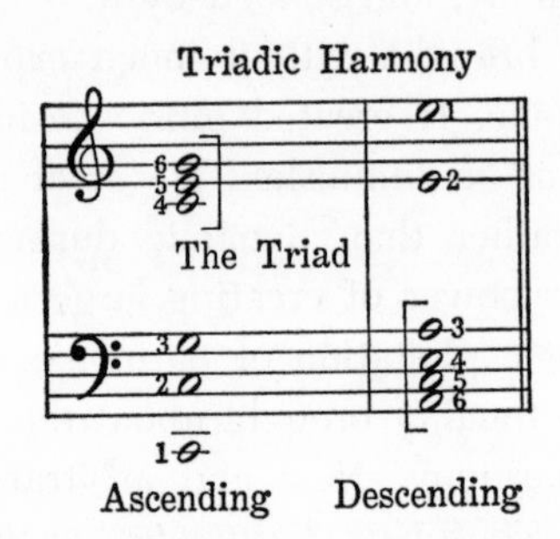

However, so long as any tones may be taken as consonant with any others, and so long as the feeling of harmony is based, as it is today, on experiments, no universally valid language can arise. The essence of any language, private meanings and associations notwithstanding, is that there is some core which means the same for all who use the language.

Perhaps it will be the task of the present generation to establish again such a language of harmony in place of antiquarian studies and merely personal experiments.

POLYPHONIC IDIOMS

Music in which two or more melodies unfold simultaneously may exhibit no resemblance at all among any of its various melodies, or varying degrees of consistency.

Imitation is that form of writing in which a specific melody or subject, stated in one voice, is reiterated more or less exactly in another. *Rounds* and *canons* are compositions in which the differerent voices sing exactly the same melody, but at different times, the parts being written to fit together. A canon is a composition, or part of a composition, in which the successive voices are identical but do not return immediately or at all to the opening subject. A round is a special form of the canon, in which the voices return shortly to their opening melody; "Three Blind Mice" exemplifies this type of composition.

Fugue is a polyphonic genre in which a melodic subject of a clear character is subject to polyphonic treatment and development of varying degrees of consistency, according to the invention of the composer. When the subject appears, it is usually imitated successively in all the other voices. It need not always be present; there are usually sections where is does not appear, termed *episodes,* which Bach considered essential for reanimating the subject. Considerations of harmony play as much a part in the fugue as do the purely melodic and polyphonic developments of the subject.

The most common treatments which polyphonic materials undergo are *augmentation,* in which the time values of the notes are multiplied; *diminution,* in which they are divided; *inversion,* in which the subject is turned upside down; and *stretto,* in which the successive entries are crowded together, so that they overlap, one voice beginning the subject before the previous voice has ended its exposition of the subject. These, in brief, are the manipulations which are the stock in trade of the textbook fugue. It may be observed that Bach wrote many a fugue in which the standard devices are barely used or not at all.

COUNTERPOINT

The term *counterpoint* refers to the pedagogical discipline of learning to write polyphony. It is a systematic series of exercises of increasing complexity, beginning with two voices in the simplest rhythms and continuing up to four or five part writing in free and complex rhythms.

The term also applies to contrapuntal writing, especially in the voices which accompany a definite subject.

Polyphony gave to music enormous resources; in fact, it transformed music. It offers the possibility to present change and repetition at the same time, variety and identity at the same moment. We are also able to hear at the same time events with which we can identify ourselves as opposed to others which, because of their pitch, range, or tempo, appear as external and objective. By polyphony a new spatial dimension was added to music—that of the juxtaposition of melodies.

The periods of our music in which polyphony was rejected or neglected have been the most impoverished; the most fertile periods have been those in which it has flourished.

CHAPTER 7

Rhythm

Perhaps rhythm should have been discussed before the other elements of music. It is a universal force, and only secondarily something musical. It is to be found in nature, in language, in the other arts, and in organic life. There is rhythm without music, but no music without rhythm.

The term, in its original Greek, means flow: a movement that surges and recedes in intensity. In this sense, even a river may be said to have rhythm. Musical rhythm is that which is comparatively regular, susceptible of simple numerical measurements. In its simplest form it is binary, the contrast between a strong and a weak pulse. If either the strong or the weak pulse is extended in time, then ternary rhythm results.

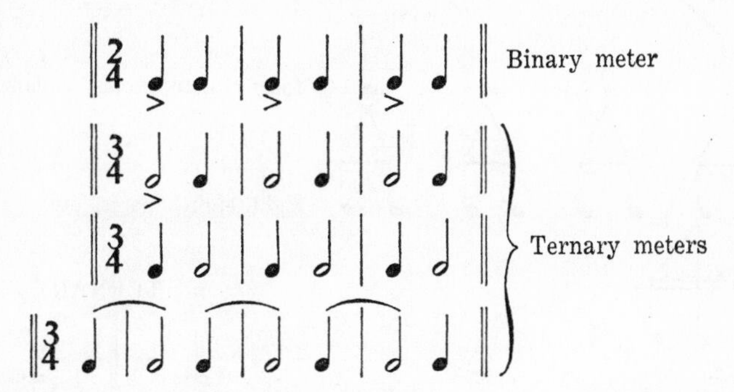

The flow of rhythm assumes many forms in music. Not only the contrast of strong and weak impulses, but also that of long and short note values, and of tones of lower and higher pitch, as well as the flow of consonant and dissonant harmonies are experienced as movements which gain or lose in intensity.

Music theory deals for the most part only with the simplest and most regular rhythmic forms—those which are called meter; the others belong to the province of the composer. Our music theory has remarkably little to say about rhythm.

METER

We have a clock built into us, the pulse, whose normal rate is about 72 beats per minute. It is by this yardstick that we judge rapid or slow events, by the extent of their departure from this tempo. The metric pulse is one, but by no means the only, component of musical rhythm.

Our music most commonly assigns the quarter note as the symbol of the metric unit. There are also note values which

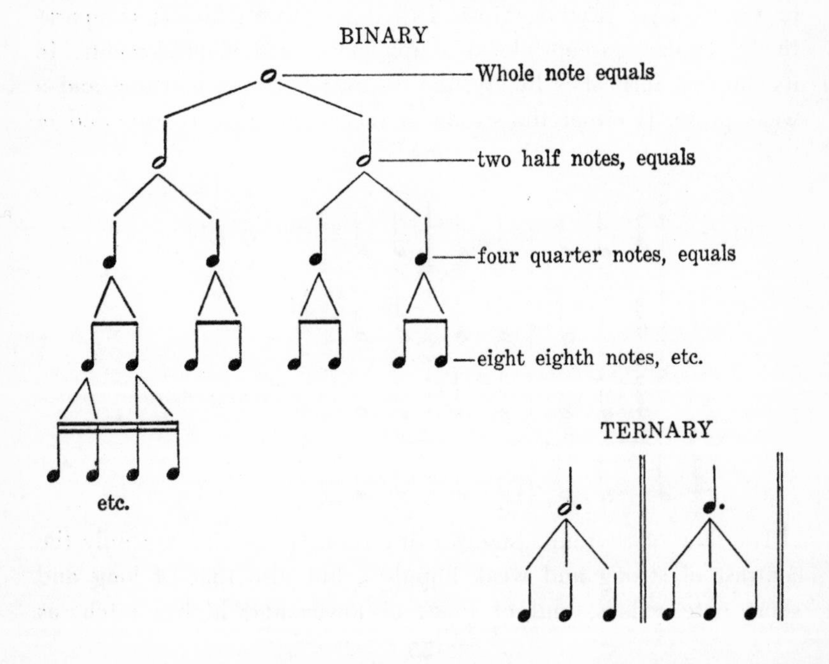

are shorter than the metric pulse, and those which are longer. Our note values are binary: each may be divided into two of the next smaller unit, and two together comprise the length of the next larger unit.

If we wish to divide our notes into three units rather than two, we use dotted notes; a dot adds one half of its value to a note. Thus, a dotted half note is equal in duration to three quarter notes instead of two, and the dotted quarter note to three eighth notes instead of two, and so on.

Much of our music, but by no means all, can be grouped into regular measures, conceived as having regularly recurring beats. Thus, in two-quarter time, two beats are counted for each measure by the performer, the first strong and the second light. In three-quarter time, three beats are counted to the measure, the first strong, the next two light.

Other note symbols may be assigned the metric pulse; we may have three-eighth time, or three-half time, and so on. The sounds of the music would be no different, only the reading.

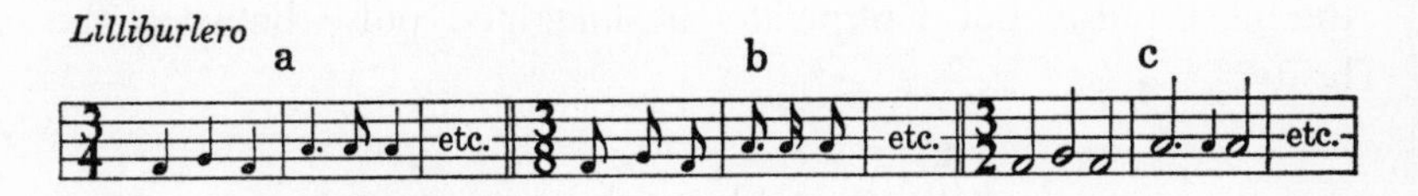

In a predominantly binary meter, occasional ternary values are indicated by triplets:

In a predominantly ternary meter, occasional binary values are indicated by duplets:

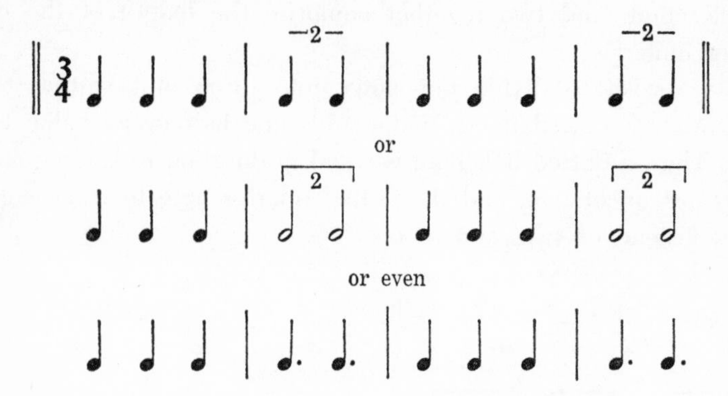

Measures of two and three are called simple meters; measures containing more beats than these are called compound. The compound meters may be said to originate by extending the speed of the metric pulse beyond the limits of tempo considered normal.

If the tempo of binary meter becomes too fast, we no longer count each beat, but shift to counting every second beat; thus:

1

etc.

1 (and) 2 (and) 1 (and) 2 (and)

Similarly, if it becomes too slow, we can no longer wait for the next pulse, but interpolate an imagined pulse between the beats.

2

etc.

1 (and) 2 (and) 1 (and) 2 (and)

In this way measures of four are developed; the first and third beats are considered strong (of the two, the first is stronger), the second and fourth, light.

If the shift of tempo is made in ternary meter, the results are somewhat different. Speeding up of the tempo will cause performers to count only the first beats of each group of three, and to group them in measures of two counts, as in 6/8 time: two beats to the measure, each beat divided into three parts. Slowing the tempo will create again an interpolation of beats; the time will remain 3/4:

1 (and) 2 (and) 3 (and)

We seem to be unable to accept a genuine meter of five beats to the measure; the beats group themselves into two plus three, or three plus two.

Measures of six may be ambiguous. If the tempo is slow and broad enough, it remains a genuine six, but if the tempo is fast, we may feel the time as binary measure, each beat divided in three:

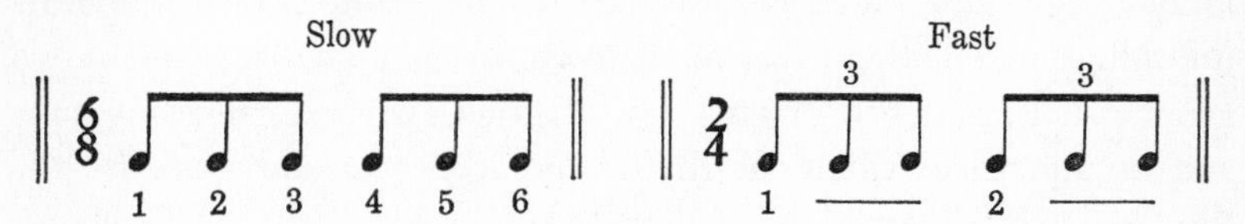

As with five, there is no meter based on seven; it breaks up into simpler components.

The only other metric values are nine and twelve to the measure. These are compound meters, not true meters in themselves. Nine is a ternary measure grouped into threes, and twelve is compound four grouped by threes:

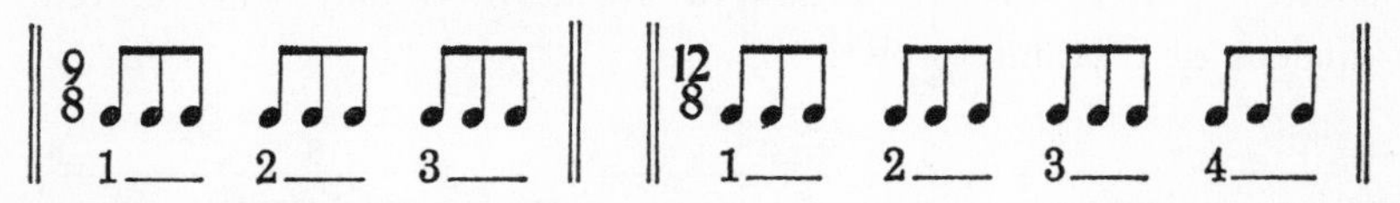

We see then that all our meters are based on simple numerical values, two and three, and that larger meters are derived from them. Such complex signatures as 10/8, 15/4, etc., are agglomerations of simpler elements.

RHYTHM

Considerations of meter are merely mechanical and have little to do with musical rhythms, which are irregular and concrete. We are normally concerned with these irregularities and not with mechanical time-beating. We are, similarly, not normally aware of our pulse beat, but of a multiplicity of organic rhythms going on simultaneously with the pulse beat: the rhythms of speech, walking, breathing, and of gesture. We experience them all together, and it is this same organic experience which makes intelligible to us the simultaneous rhythms of harmonic dissonances and consonances, long and short note values, and melodic *motifs* and gestures.

Meter corresponds to time, which is in fact an unbroken and unmeasured flow; it needs, as Aristoxenus states, the temporal unfolding of something real for its own articulation. The equal and symmetrical values of meter are abstract, whereas the unequal and asymmetrical values of rhythm are concrete and give rise to the former by abstraction.

There are innumerable rhythms that can be devised to fill out the skeleton of the meter and there exists no theoretical classification of them.

THE RHYTHMIC MOTIF

A rhythmic motif is a short, concise rhythmic pattern, the shortest pattern that is meaningful by itself. It may serve as the nucleus of rhythmic growth.

The rhythmic motif shows a short value moving to a long, heavy value; this pattern repeats itself on a large as well as a small scale. The rhythm is consistent but not mechanical. Variety enters at points of articulation, that is, at the end of phrases.

MUSICAL PHRASES AND SENTENCES

The normal musical sentence is that of eight measures, frequently but not necessarily divided in two half sentences of four measures each. (See example immediately above.) There are, to be sure, sentences or phrases that are shorter and longer; these are brought about by elisions or overlappings, or by extensions, repetitions, or expansions. Eight measures is the norm.

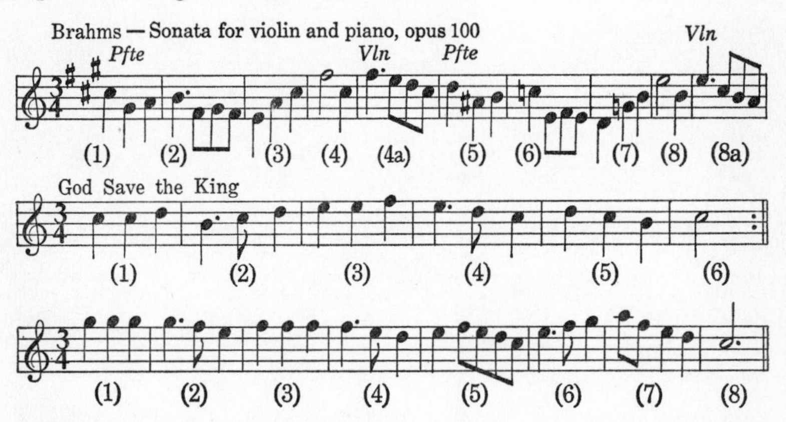

With concrete motifs and phrases, rhythm becomes bound up with melody, and it becomes difficult to separate the two; the motif is both rhythmic and melodic at the same time.

Music theory has given as little attention to rhythm as it has to melody. There seem to exist definite types of rhythmic formation, but their discovery and elaboration are still left to the composer and theory is unable to separate general laws from the various personal styles of individual artists. At present, the most general features are those of meter, which are the stable elements of rhythm, in contrast to the specific formations by individual composers.

Part Three

THE PRACTICE OF MUSIC

CHAPTER 8

Music as Part of Our Civilization

Creation

Today we find a rather sharp distinction made in musical life between creating music, performing it, and listening to it. One man writes music, another plays it, and a third listens to it—all quite separate activities. It is possible to be professionally distinguished in one of these fields—as composer, performer, or critic—without being especially skillful in any of the others. Good composers have been bad performers and critics, and the same may be said for each of the other métiers.

Such separation of functions is a recent development; originally the creation and performance of music were one and the same event, known as improvisation. This kind of music making, which exists today as something vestigial, was the principal way of making music in the ancient world. We know that much ancient music consisted of standard melodic patterns. The Greeks termed them *nomoi;* in India, they were termed *ragas,* and by scholars of Hebrew music, *motives.* The same system has been observed even in the earliest music of the West, in Gregorian chant, and among other nations as well. The characteristic trait of this ancient music is that it consists of standard patterns, usually fairly brief, which are of anonymous origin and the common property of musicians.

Musicians composed by putting these standard patterns together in one or another order. Like the jazz musicians of today, they worked with melodic material which everyone in the audience knew, materials learned by the members of the community from their earliest years. Our popular music and folk music still retain most of the main features of music making in the ancient world, improvisation playing a major part. Improvisation as an art depends upon the performer possessing a repertoire of musical formulas. He improvises by varying or embellishing his stock material according to the inspiration of the moment. If inspiration happens to be lacking, he is always able to fall back on a standard formula. Furthermore, the distinction between performers and audience is much less clear. In the ancient world, listening from a detached point of view was somewhat irrelevant, unless perhaps the listener was a deity being invoked. We may recall the antiphonal method of singing psalms in Old Testament times. The leader would sing one line of the psalm, and the congregation would respond either by repeating that line or a part of it, or by singing the next line of the psalm. Community participation was the normal practice.

Not only was there no evidence of the distinctions which we find so sharply made in Western music, but distinctions between music and poetry, and music and the dance were not made. The Greek term for music, *mousike,* meant, first of all, intellectual life in general, and secondly, "words and music" and "dance and music." Music by itself was considered meaningless. It is almost impossible to separate such music from the enactment of some myth or legend.

Throughout the ancient world, the standard musical forms were identified with cosmic forces: seasons of the year, fire, cold, water, wind, the signs of the Zodiac, and so on. Such a musical conception survives today in the liturgy of the church, with its calendar of Gregorian chants suitable for particular days of the year and for particular occasions. Such identification is the musical expression of the ancient unity of man's mind with the forces of nature and his unquestioning acceptance of his limited but fixed place in the cosmos. Such a view is in contrast to the modern conception of man's mind as being more or less separated from nature and more or less liberated from it, and is related to the modern conception of music as an art autonomous of the other arts, finding its values within itself alone.

The symbolism of ancient art, which identified the materials of art with universal forces, may stand in danger of being misunderstood by the modern reader, who may see in it something akin to program music—imitations or portrayals by means of music. Such a conception is far removed from the ancient one, which was symbolism of a high order. For the ancients, the musical materials were symbols of these forces, entities which fused two regions into one reality.

No one knows the historical origins of music making. But we may observe our children turning speech into song and movement into dance, as a result of heightened energy and emotion, and we may suppose that music originated in this way, as a dimension added to something else. Music in its origins may be conceived as the immediate utterance of a state of mind, of enhanced psychic and physical energy; it may be made to coincide with the desire for communication, and frequently does, though it need not.

Later music became not only the immediate utterance of a state of mind but also the means for inducing this same state of mind. Ancient literature is filled with tales of the effect of music on the mind. The prophets called for music that they might be able to prophesy and the mentally ill were said to be healed by musical means: in this way did David heal Saul.

The occasions for music making in the ancient world were mainly communal, occurring mostly at the religious rites which constituted their societies, those events clearly related to the life of the community—warfare, planting and harvesting, births and deaths.

Musical life today is something radically different. A steady development persisting for more than two thousand years has changed completely our view of music and musicians. Music has evolved steadily toward an autonomous state. The highest achievements of our musical art are instrumental compositions performed for their own sake, without literary or religious connections. The music needs no meaning attached to it; the meaning is in the music itself.

Of course music is still performed at worship, at places of work, and is used for marching, but these are mostly decayed vestiges. Such music is not considered the summit of our musical art and is rather dependent upon musical life going on elsewhere. A glance at a modern hymnal shows music mostly borrowed from the classical repertoire of instrumental music: minuets from symphonies, excerpts from piano sonatas, and so on. Popular music has shown itself to be highly dependent upon harmonic developments which come from outside itself and has made no contributions to music theory. The high points of the music of the past two centuries have been in such autonomous fields as the instrumental sonata, the string quartet, and the symphony.

Improvisation still survives in popular music, and perhaps the only survival of community participation in music, using materials learned by the audience in childhood, is the Protestant hymn tune, the chorale. Many of these hymn tunes are still well known. "Old Hundred" and "A Mighty Fortress Is Our God" are sung today, and many others. Many of them had once been popular tunes which were taken over for religious usage, there being no reason, as Luther put it, for the devil to have all the good tunes. Isaac's "O Innsbruck I Must Leave Thee" took on a different cast with the words "O World I Must Leave Thee." Thus, by their origins and by their usage, these tunes were known to all the congregation, who could sing them by heart. The chorale prelude for organ existed as a kind of musical commentary on the chorale melody. It was often enough improvisatory in character, but whether improvised or composed, it was designed as an expansion and reworking of preexistent material of common property, according to the ancient conception, with the purpose of elevating the listener's mind and feelings to the religious matters at hand.

Popular music and folk music are the living heirs of this older conception of making music by improvising on preexistent materials. Scholars have demonstrated for contemporary English and American folk music the same traits: the diffusion over the English-speaking world of a very limited number of melodic shapes—about forty—which account for almost all of its folk melodies.

Improvisation in art music has all but died out. Most piano or violin concertos, for example, have a section set aside for the performer in which the orchestra stops completely, leaving the soloist free to display his invention by improvising on the principal melodies of the concerto, but composers long ago found performers unreliable in this respect, and were forced to write out these cadenzas for them. Formerly there also existed a kind of musical shorthand, called figured bass, from which keyboard players were expected to perform *extempore,* but this technique too has died out, and modern editions have to write out the shorthand for the keyboard player. The improvisatory side of art music is an archaic trait, as is the connection of music with concrete meanings and images. The whole development of music has been toward an autonomous state needing no literary or religious context to give it significance.

THE PLACE OF THE MUSICIAN IN SOCIETY

The social position of musicians has also changed. The musician of the ancient world was an anonymous figure whose creation coincided with his performance. He improvised casually and ephemerally on known melodies which were usually sacred, of great antiquity, but of mythical origins. The beginnings of Greek music were characteristically ascribed to legendary figures, Orpheus, Apollo, Olympus. The development of Western music, and specifically of Western polyphony, has conditioned the emergence of composition as a distinct accomplishment and consequently of the composer as a distinct person, working within a musical tradition, but making individual and original contributions. For most of the period of music history there was no individually composed music, written down. Most music was simply what one folk musician picked up from another, with no idea whatever—or perhaps only a hazy one—that written music existed. It is only on the threshold of our own era that musicians speak of a composition as a *res facta*—a thing which has been made. It was made and recorded in its own notation, the esoteric property of a distinct professional figure.

The musician as a professional person appeared first as a monk, later as a functionary attached either to a church or to the retinue of some nobleman, and still later as a craftsman free to seek employment with a municipality, a church, or a court. It was not until the latter part of the nineteenth century that the musician, and more specifically, the composer, began to assume a status similar to that of other professionals. It is of interest to note that although the composer today has a somewhat higher stature, he seems to have become somewhat less free concerning the content of his music. Haydn and Mozart, though they ate with the servants, were free from the point of view of musical styles. Twentieth century composers, though they are honored professional men, are much more circumscribed. Since the late nineteenth century, the musical world, like all other branches of intellectual life, has become increasingly political in atmosphere, and in some countries even the musical substance of a composition is scrutinized carefully from a rather political point of view. Robert Schumann wrote that a revolution could be contained within the four walls of a symphony and the police be none the wiser. Those days seem to be gone. Where the composer is not directly under political supervision, he is often as rigidly watched by the polemical critics of one or another school of composing. The polemical spirit of politics seems to have entered the field of musical composition with Wagner and his followers, who in their writings raised the banner of "progressive" as opposed to "reactionary" composing, a concept which, whatever its virtues for politics, clouds our understanding of musical life. While it is true that in some periods of music history the great figures were the innovators, the "progressives," there are as many instances to be seen when the composers of lasting significance were conservatives, or "reactionaries," and when the innovators produced music of ephemeral value which led nowhere.

There seems always to have existed a rather wide difference between the status of the official musician of church, court, or university and the secular musician of the people, the exponent of popular music. The official composers were frequently men of rank in the church; some were granted patents of nobility. But the official world has never been sympathetic to the tavern, the dance hall, or the theater, and has invariably treated their musical representatives with scant justice. Popular musicians of the street and tavern suffered ill-treatment and ill-repute, even as they do today. Yet they are significant, if in no other way, as the exponents of music making as it was in older times. Even into the twentieth century, street and tavern singers, often blind like Homer, served as a kind of newspaper and political commentary, composing musical observations on the events of the day. Until the advent of mass literacy they, like the old bards, served a real function in the lives of the people. Nursery tunes and nursery rhymes to this day are filled with the half-remembered commentaries on political events which occurred centuries ago, and even today musical skits composed on contemporary figures can arouse feelings almost forgotten.

Although the composer and musician are in a somewhat ambiguous position today, a definite trend in the history of music may be observed. Composers of the Middle Ages and after were mostly in the employ of the church or the court, or both. They were commissioned to write music for specific occasions: religious services at a cathedral or the chapel of a nobleman and secular pieces for entertainments. Later, composers were employed by townships. Music was made mostly for specific practical occasions and with specific performers in mind. It was a job to be done by a qualified craftsman with no ambitions to write immortal music. By the seventeenth and eighteenth centuries the increasing secularization of Western society may be observed in music by the gradual drift of composers away from the church and toward such secular fields as the theater. In the eighteenth century something new emerged: an independent concert life. Musicians were now able to seek their living by performing or even by publishing and selling their music. The masterworks were no longer reserved only to those having access to the salons or chapels of a nobleman but became more or less available to anyone with the price of a ticket. J. S. Bach, whose sacred music constitutes a large proportion of his total output, was among the last of the great masters to earn his living as a church composer and even he was something of an anachronism in his own day. The sacred music of later masters, though valuable, is not a major part of their production, and usually is not even suitable for religious services. Beethoven's *Missa Solemnis* or Verdi's *Requiem* go far beyond the limits of the most solemn liturgical occasion, and even Bach's cantatas were bitterly resented at the St. Thomas Church as being unsuitable for worship. Now they are frequently to be heard in churches, but their performance there merely indicates that the churches have learned to conform to the usages of concert life; liturgical music itself is sadly deteriorated.

Since the nineteenth century, the practice of writing music for specific occasions, sacred or secular, has all but disappeared (except for the considerable body of music every generation creates for teaching purposes), and composers today write for no specific occasions. A musician today may write a symphony or a string quartet, and with luck will hear it once or twice in his lifetime. But the composer as craftsman, paid for his skill, has disappeared. He earns his living by something else, and composes on his own time, out of his own initiative.

This is a significant development, but not all that it signifies is beneficial to musical life. For centuries music was used only with the other arts, and of course still serves to heighten the effects of poetry, drama, religious services, and so on, but was not generally recognized as having a specific intellectual significance of its own. Writings about music are full of references to the power of music to rouse the passions—these being neatly labeled and classified—and to quiet the mind, or to more vague discussions of beauty, inspiration, and so forth. But at last music has emerged as something existing in its own right, in which association with other arts is something secondary. Music is performed today with a complete disregard of practical occasions; one may hear at the same recital a motet, a cantata, a serenade, and even music from an opera. Such mixtures are a little disturbing and suggest that the music is being enjoyed as museum pieces are enjoyed: that is, no longer as a part of human life. But they also mean of course that the music has a timeless value over and above that of its intended function, a value which is best comprehended in a purely musical occasion.

The disappearance of the composer as a craftsman paid to exercise his skill is on one hand a gain, at least in indicating his rise in stature to that of the literary or professional figure, but on the whole a great loss, both for the composer and for musical life in general.

When the composer held a specific post as court, church, or town musician, he enjoyed certain valuable advantages, over and above that of being paid to be a musician. He had a specific audience; composer and audience knew each other and over the course of the years had ample opportunity to grow and learn. The audience, in the process, often came to recognize and to expect high value. Haydn and Beethoven were especially fortunate in this respect and by no means exceptional. The composer was faced with an obligation both to himself and to his audience. He was free to grow and to experiment, to be original, but at the same time was obliged to make himself intelligible to his audience. There was often enough conflict between these two obligations—Bach's relations with his employers were often quite bad, Mozart's music was much more than the superficial entertainment desired by the aristocracy and he suffered for it, Brahms's achievement was not fully comprehended by the educated German middle class to which he addressed his music—but the need to resolve this conflict seems to be the best discipline for the artist. In twentieth century musical life, where the composer has only an anonymous mass audience and where his opportunities for performances are comparatively rare, he tends either to devote himself entirely to original experiments with little or no concern for intelligibility, or to write music which is immediately striking and pleasing. In either case his work suffers: in the first, his music becomes so private and personal as to be unintelligible, not only to the audience of laymen, but even to the educated professional musicians who perform it; in the second, the work usually is without lasting value.

His role, then, as an isolated literary figure, is somewhat unfortunate. Music seems to have been greatly influenced by the example of Beethoven, who was forced by his deafness to give up musical performing and to try to live by his composing. It seems best for the composer to remain as close as possible to practical music making. All the masters of the past have been at least competent performers. They usually began as part of a going concern, a choir or an orchestra, and after an apprenticeship found themselves supplying music for it. The disappearance of these conditions is due partly to the decline of churches, courts, and townships as supporters of musical life. Nothing has appeared so far to replace them except the international concert industry, which is both passive and completely sterile as far as musical developments are concerned; it is willing to exploit past achievements but offers nothing to contemporary developments. It is conceivable that the universities may arise as important supporters of music. A number of European and American composers today are connected with universities, but only as teachers. Their specific function as composers and practical musicians has little place in the university. The universities themselves are not certain that practical music, as distinguished from the historical discipline of musicology, is a liberal art or has a legitimate place in the liberal arts curriculum. The writing and playing of music is left mostly to the conservatory and the music school. Unfortunately these latter tend mostly to prepare young persons for the concert industry—they turn out excellently trained young virtuosi and in fact many more than can actually earn their livelihood in music—who generally have not much connection with the intellectual currents of university life.

Practical performing has a place beside musicology in the university. Musicology first rose to significance in the latter part of the nineteenth century and since has exerted a significant influence on musical life. It has deciphered old manuscripts of music whose notation until recently was a dead language, and has thereby restored to life many masterpieces. In one respect, musicology represents a major achievement of the twentieth century: in all previous eras men knew only the music of their own generation and perhaps that of the generation just before theirs. More often than not, a composer's music disappeared from practical performance after his death and only a few figures of exceptional stature were remembered. Musicology has given to musicians a large perspective over the the full evolution of music, and particular figures and styles may be seen within the scope of a long historical process.

This development too has its dangers; audiences and performers tend to prefer music from the past that is safely certified as great music and avoid contact with the men of their own generation. Everyone is impoverished by this and the average musician and scholar usually has lost the capacity to comprehend the truly important events of his own generation. Another danger of too much historical awareness is the error of trying to anticipate or force new developments. Freakish experiments and cynical incomprehensibilities can always be offered as the next stage of development; originality can be claimed to be important, and there are always those willing to say anything in order to be original. Finally there is the danger of thinking that works are created in order to be part of a historical process or even by means of the consciousness of history. Art is created by other forces altogether. Its creations exist in their own right, not in order to be part of a historical pageant, and they are sure to bear the marks of their time and place without any conscious designs on the part of their creators.

These difficulties notwithstanding, it should be the duty of the universities to provide some living repository for the achievements of the past, the *Collegium Musicum,* in which the great works of *all* eras, not just those of the distant past, receive live performances.

We should understand that a museum is the repository of the highest achievements of past eras—those achievements of timeless value—but *not* of everything.

Musicology is in this respect perhaps unable to help. It has performed a great service in excavating and deciphering the gigantic mass of music of past eras. But musicology as such is unable to sort out from this vast mass those works which are significant works of art. It has never been a condition for the existence of music that it must be significant as art, nor should it be, and only in exceptional cases does it achieve this state. The selection of such works can only be made by practical musicians devoted to performing these works. If a piece of music has an inherent vitality, it becomes self-sustaining, finds itself being performed again and again. If not, it will simply disappear. The world of concert life, and the record business, are unable to perform these functions. It would seem that the logical place for this living museum is the university, once it becomes clear that music is indeed a liberal art and possesses intellectual significance.

PERFORMANCE

The performer today is a professional figure of a high order of skill. In the past hundred years or so there has occurred a truly remarkable rise in the quality of performance. There are today a host of performers, obscure and undistinguished, whose playing would have created a sensation a century ago.

This rise in the standards of performance is due to several factors: to increased demands made by composers, to structural changes in musical instruments, to the rise of the international concert and recording industries, and to the impact of the touring virtuosi and conductors of the nineteenth and early twentieth centuries. Styles of composing and the designs of instruments have sometimes had a reciprocal influence. Beethoven's powerful piano style actually called into being a series of structural changes in the piano itself;

the transformed piano in turn made possible the pianistic styles of such later composers as Liszt, Brahms, and Debussy. The interest in harmony and modulation led to innovations in wind instruments that greatly extended their capacities; these increased capacities in turn led to the newer styles of twentieth century orchestration, in which wind instruments play a much greater part.

THE PERFORMER AS CRAFTSMAN AND ARTIST

The performer is one who must know well both his instrument and the composition he performs. His tasks do not end with mastery of the technical difficulties of playing his instrument or of specific compositions. Such mastery is a prerequisite to his professional career. His task is to make himself the vehicle of the music he performs. The masterworks need lifelong study and consideration.

A great deal is said and written in this respect about what is falsely called the "interpretation" of music, a term misleading to performers and public alike. Musical compositions may be regarded as vehicles for one or another performing personality, having no interest or value otherwise. The famous "interpretations" by these personalities are usually a set of arbitrary mannerisms—distorted tempos, portentous inflections of volume, the so-called rich tone—imposed upon the music and unrelated to its structure. Performers frequently trade upon their mannerisms.

Such tendencies are as old as concert life. They were enhanced by the performing personalities of the romantic era, Paganini, Liszt, Rubinstein, Nikisch, and many others, and have been more or less standardized by the concert and record industries, eager to sell another "interpretation" to the not too well oriented mass audience. Now, a large body of music has been written expressly for performers, expressly to communicate the player's mastery of his instrument. Some of it is fine music, but the masterworks, by and large, have not been written with such a purpose in mind. For these compositions, it is sufficient to read and perform the notes accurately. The greatest performer is the one who makes us forget his presence. And the basis for such performing is not a set of personal mannerisms for distorting the music but a faithful and accurate reading of the notes. This is the foundation of all performing.

> Notable as a characteristic of contemporary American orchestral style is the systematic employment of forced tone, of overbowing and overblowing . . . Paris, London, Vienna, and Berlin have always operated on the assumption that auditory beauty (and, indeed, expression) diminishes where forced tone begins . . . , exaggerated dynamic impact being considered as a sort of bluff, a playing to the audience's grosser nervous and emotional reactions in lieu of making specific sense—what the theatrical world calls *ham.*
>
> Many American soldiers have spoken to me about what they consider the low general standard of execution at French orchestral concerts. Accustomed to a high polish in performance, they are shocked at its absence. The younger ones, of course, don't know that French taste has never considered a high polish essential to first class workmanship. . . . They work from the inside out, believing that correct phraseology, appropriately varied coloration, and exact balances, will produce live music and that live music needs no makeup. Its natural bloom is considered to be sufficient. . . . we need to be reminded again about the relative importance of interior equilibrium in music as against luxury surfacing. Also of the increased expressivity that comes of eschewal of all passional camouflage, particularly that of forced tone.*

The performing virtuosi of the romantic era were in their own way great creative figures; their skills were an expression of a vitality of the same order as that which goes into the composition of music. They often put themselves at the service of the best composers and were quite worthy of the glory they gained, but as ends in themselves they did not help concert life and lost touch with important developments. Whereas once they were in the *avant-garde* of the best music of their time as, for example, Joachim and Clara Schumann with respect to Brahms, or Liszt with Chopin, today the performer is the captive of the concert business, repeating over and over again a limited, old repertoire.

* Virgil Thomson, "From Overseas," November 25, 1945, in *The Art of Judging Music,* pp. 230-231 (New York, 1948).

PERFORMANCE PRACTICE

The performer's task, that of doing justice to the composition, is not always an easy one. Assuming that he is musically educated, knowing well the music theory of his own time and of past eras, and is consequently able to comprehend a composition, he now encounters some of the great puzzles of music. He discovers that composers, for the most part, have been remarkably reticent concerning the performance of their music. One hardly knows for sure the intended tempo of a piece, which parts to play loud or soft, or how to articulate the melodies—which notes are to be linked to their neighbors, which detached. The greatest composers especially, who were such painstaking masters of their craft, appear to have been remarkably indifferent to this side of the music, leaving only the barest hints or, more frequently, none at all. This puzzle may be explained to a large extent by the former social conditions of music; most music was written by composers for ensembles to which they belonged, with no intention of writing for a wider audience or for posterity. There was no need to write in performance indications that everyone in the group knew, and if some question arose the composer was always there to answer it. Even when the music was widely disseminated, it was disseminated within a profession having a common living tradition. It would not have occurred to musicians to write down a living language—everyone in the profession knew it by practice.

But of course the modern performer is in no such position. Musicians have rediscovered works that have lain neglected for centuries and they have become interested in music outside their own national traditions. Thus the music of distant times or distant nations often poses a serious problem to the performer, who may wonder if the instruments he knows, their modes of articulation, and even the very pitch and tone quality they can produce, at all resemble the sounds originally expected by the composer. There is, to be sure, plenty of evidence that these things have changed with the years. The pianist who buys an accurate edition of the

Beethoven piano sonatas, assuming that one exists, finds little more than the barest notes and only the most sketchy indications of dynamics and phrasing. If he turns to the music of Bach, he finds no indications whatever. He will find the music filled with strange and controversial symbols—ornaments—and will find considerable argument among scholars as to how they were meant to be played. It is dangerous for him to look into source books. He might look into the treatise on playing keyboard instruments by Bach's son Carl Philip Emanuel, which includes a thorough discussion of ornaments, but he would be misled, since the son's discussion cannot be applied to the older man's music. Father and son belonged to rather different schools of composition, as well as to different eras. Our pianist may also learn that certain rhythmic patterns—dotted notes for example—had a slightly different meaning in Bach's time than they have today.

Similarly, the conductor who prepares one of Bach's cantatas for performance will discover trumpet parts which his trumpeters simply cannot play well. Their extreme difficulty has given rise to the speculation that either there existed in Bach's time special trumpets which have fallen out of use or that the trumpeters of that time possessed unique skills which have disappeared. In either event, the conductor must resign himself to a faulty realization of the music.

Some of Beethoven's symphonies suffer from the limitations of the horns in his time, which were restricted to a few tonalities. This means that a theme given early in a work to the horns must be given to other instruments when the theme returns in another key, with a loss of character. A case can be made for some reorchestrating, now that horns can play in almost any key.

The choral conductor who prepares music by Renaissance composers is faced with similar puzzles. The sources of the music normally give only the bare notes; the words are often printed separately. For a long time it was maintained that all early music was performed purely *a cappella,* that is, sung without any instrumental accompaniment. Such contemporary decriptions as have been discovered, and especially Renaissance paintings that depict musical performances, almost invariably indicate that the singers were accompanied and sometimes replaced by instruments. The *a cappella* ideal of singing seems to have held sway in a much narrower period of music history than was once believed.

The performer of early music must also face the problem of what is called *musica ficta:* many sharps or flats were not written into the music because the singers were expected to know when to apply them. Although some practical rules have come down to us, there are many passages in which the application of *musica ficta,* or the failure to apply it, can lead to disputes as complicated as any theological argument.

Performers know also that certain liberties could be taken with musical rhythm—Mozart speaks of *tempo rubato* in a letter as something fairly obvious—but the whole idea of taking such liberties is a dangerous one; one cannot tell when they might be misapplied by performers.

The researches of musicologists have done a great deal in this respect—though often enough they have been able to tell us only how much we do *not* know—but even if research could uncover the most complete details of performance practice, the performer's task would not be solved. The reticence of the composer with respect to the details of performing is only partially explained by reference to the social conditions of music. Even composers such as Beethoven, Chopin, and Brahms, who lived by their composing and who consequently expected their works to be published far and wide among amateurs as well as among professionals, display this same negligence with respect to the details of performance. The puzzle lies to a large extent beyond the reach of historical considerations.

Perhaps the safest approach is to say that the composers knew that detailed indications are superfluous to those performers who know what they are about and useless for those who do not. In practice, every performer has to shape the music in the light of his own grasp of the unwritten language, and the art of performance *is* an unwritten language. The trouble is that some conceptions of this language are better than others. The true art of performing is an art of articulation and phrasing, but it is apparently something that cannot be formulated in concrete terms. The performer who knows this art may take liberties in the service of the music; he who does not is in danger of simulating it by arbitrary distortions, like the actor who announces everything, even the most trivial pronouncements, in a voice quavering with simulated emotion and unnatural inflections. Because of this danger, the safest procedure for the performer—and the surest approach to an understanding of this language—is simply to read the notes accurately and evenly, and to let such "expression" as is to be applied grow out of his improving understanding and conception of the music.

At any given moment, one may espy two features in a composition: the idea which carries it forward and that material which accompanies. The test of the performer is his ability to perceive and to indicate in his playing just where the leading voice is, as distinguished from the rest which just follows.

Such a mode of performing—the accurate and straightforward reading of the notes, coupled with a seeking out of the leading idea—will never violate the music, as does the arbitrary "expression" that is poured indiscriminately over the music like theatrical make-up.

MUSICAL EDITIONS

Music publishing until recently was not especially faithful to the composer's indications. It was fashionable in the nineteenth century to publish standard works such as the Beethoven piano sonatas with editorial indications by one or another distinguished performer, a practice still prevalent today. Each commercial publishing house offered editions by a leading virtuoso of the day, with indications for performance down to the last detail of fingering, phrasing, and dynamics.

Such editions were published, and survive, in response to the interest of a widespread public eager to know and study these works. But while the desire for guidance in these matters is legitimate, the results are not. The editors abused their privileges dreadfully; they were not careful to distinguish their indications from those of the composer, if indeed they preserved the latter at all; and because so many of these editors considered the works as vehicles for their performing, they felt free to eliminate parts from the original, to add to it, and to change it. The harmonic tastes of the romantic period found older music too thin and pale and found it desirable to add thicker, more sonorous harmonies to the music. These defacements became so common that by the end of the nineteenth century and well into our own time the commercial editions had become completely unreliable. One scholar brought out an edition of the Beethoven piano sonatas with the somewhat bitter remark, "as reconstructed from the manuscripts and the first editions." A strong reaction set in toward accuracy and our own time has seen a great labor performed in providing accurate, reliable editions, without any editorial indications other than those of the composer, or with such indications carefully distinguished. Some of the abuses remain uncorrected and in the case of Chopin's music, the tangle may never be solved. The first reliable edition of Mozart's piano sonatas, offering only genuine works by Mozart and only the notes as he wanted them, appeared in 1956. Even the editions of Beethoven's music are subject to controversy. The music of Haydn, like that of the earlier masters of the Baroque and Renaissance periods, resembles the settlement of America in the seventeenth century: partially explored, with only a general idea of its full extent.

Nevertheless, some of these old editions do have something positive about them (especially some of von Bülow's editions of Beethoven). They testify, at least, that the performer should make decisions and that even a mistaken decision is better than timid correctness, so long as it comes from the intention to make the musical structure clear. Furthermore, many of these works contain great technical difficulties and one must respect the suggestions of those who have mastered them. Finally, many of the editors were gifted men whose editions and performances did occasionally represent a thoughtful response to the works they were playing.

By and large, however, such responses cannot be written down; they belong only to performance itself and perhaps to phonograph records, but not to editions of the music.

THE TRANSCRIPTION OF MUSIC

The rise of historical research and a certain reaction against arbitrarily distorted performance have encouraged a trend toward performing music as far as possible with literal accuracy and complete faithfulness to the letter of the law. There are persons who will not listen to Bach performed on the piano, who insist upon the performance *a cappella* of all sixteenth century music, and who generally object to any music transcribed, orchestrated, or rearranged in any way. To this way of thinking is due in large part the revival of old or obsolete instruments, the restoration to the organ of older and simpler registrations, and the revival of the harpsichord and clavichord. Much good has been accomplished in this way, but these revivals, and the pedantic literalness they express, tend to ignore just that which is timeless in music. If the beauties of the music can be perceived in the score itself, not much of significance will be added by reviving shawms, pommers, serpents, and cromornes, unless our age discovers its own use for these instruments.

Both tendencies, that of "interpretation" and that of perfect historical accuracy, express a certain confusion about performance. This is not to say that there is a middle ground between literal accuracy and personal arbitrariness, but rather to say that there is one side of the music toward which the performer has to be faithful and self-effacing, and another side toward which he is not only free to make decisions, but even obliged to do so. A composition is, on one side, an intellectual structure. Toward this side composers have been painstaking craftsman, devoting to it thought and skill with great patience. On another side, this structure is embodied in sound, and toward this side composers have been comparatively free. Bach called his forty-eight preludes and fugues *The Well-Tempered Key-*

board, evidently not concerned too much with just which keyboard—organ, harpsichord, piano, or clavichord—played them. He transcribed and arranged much music, his own and that of other composers, from one medium to another with great freedom. Beethoven arranged one of his own piano sonatas for string quartet, with the idea of showing the plagiarists who pirated and rearranged his compositions how to do it correctly. Renaissance music, we know, was performed by whatever was available—voices, instruments, or both—and Elizabethan madrigals appeared with the inscription "apt for voices or viols."

Composers appear not to be much concerned with the sound of music itself. Certainly pitch has been a chaos over the years—instruments have varied in pitch in every country and in every generation—until it was standardized in the nineteenth century. Some composers have been somewhat indifferent orchestrators, most notably Schumann, Chopin, and Bruckner, and a good case could be made for improving their scoring. The controversial changes in some of Bruckner's symphonies, made with his consent by his disciples, have something to recommend them despite the claim of defacement made against them. The difficulty with all such changes and liberties is that it depends on who does them. The old saying, *Quod licet Jovi, non licet bovi* (What Jupiter may do, the cattle may not) still applies here. The difficulty, again, is the natural tendency of performers, arrangers, and especially conductors, to place themselves in the first category instead of the second.

The performer is free to make use of whatever resources of sound he may have available for the purpose of making clear the structure of the music.

The primary source for the details of performance practice is in the composition itself, and not in historic research into contemporary sources, of doubtful value. The rigid application of such research to performance, while often valuable, more frequently has the effect of the cosmetic art of the mortuary than of living art. The primary source, it must be repeated, is the composition itself, and the first arbiter of performing decisions is the practical musician, rather than the research scholar.

Listening to Music

There are not only professional composers and performers but professional listeners as well: reviewers of music and records. The music critic came into existence only at the end of the eighteenth century and the beginning of the nineteenth, coinciding with the rise and triumph of public concert life. He serves, apparently, as mediator between the professional musicians and the broader public that came to support music in place of the churches and nobles. It is, so it seems, his task to report excellence, either of composition or of performance, to the public at large. Unfortunately, when measured by the standards of history, his own performance is not very good. There have been a few good critics—most notably Schumann, Berlioz, and Hanslick. The rest, with astonishing consistency, have ignored or condemned the important achievements of their time and have praised and encouraged developments which have long since been forgotten. This is a performance consistent with that of all journalism but it is not a musical function.

The poverty of critical performance is due chiefly to the critics' application of standards to the wrong party. They have, according to their lights, sought to chastise composers and performers and have thus stood as partisans of the public—a public not very well educated. Their real function should be to address their standards to the public and to seek to raise general standards of musical education and perception. Too many members of our audiences know that Haydn and Mozart are great artists; they know it in the same way that they know the distance from the earth to the sun: they have it on good authority. But it is questionable how many listeners experience directly that which makes great the works of these men, how many perceive just what the composers' virtues are, and the difference between good and bad. Apparently few listeners care to explore music that might turn out to be less than the best; rather than trust their responses they turn to the critical reviews. This, in fact, is the function of musical journalism.

The intrusion of critics into musical tendencies and the currents of musical history has not been constructive. Musical life, as all intellectual life, should be left free to reflect and dispose of the intellectual currents of an era according to their inherent vitality. Very few members of any generation are able to judge accurately in these matters, as the bad performance of criticism indicates, and such judgments represent an intrusion into regions which by right are autonomous.

The basic function of music criticism should be the raising of public standards and the development of musical aesthetics. Criticism should be able to demonstrate the particular virtues or defects of a given composition and to devise and formulate generally valid musical standards. Some valuable works have been written on musical aesthetics—Hanslick's treatise *On the Beautiful in Music* is one of them—but these presuppose a well developed understanding of music; they are not introductions. There does not exist a literature of music criticism, comparable to literary criticism, that makes detailed aesthetic investigations of individual works. It may perhaps develop, but if it does it will probably be as far removed from the reviewing of concerts as literary studies are from the reviewing of books.

Our musical life today is not healthy. Certainly our composers do not think that it is, nor do the professional performers, both those who have managed to survive and those who have been forced into other fields by the phonograph record and concert industries.

> . . . Dozens of handsomely equipped artists never obtain a toehold in the field simply because they have no way of obtaining engagements.
>
> The concert business is dreadfully overcrowded. In addition to the established performers–Jascha Heifetz, Artur Rubenstein, Marian Anderson, Lily Pons, and colleagues only a little less successful—quantities of less celebrated artists are seeking to carve out careers. Young musicians pour into the profession in a floodstream from the colleges, conserva-

tories and studios, where they have been encouraged (frequently by unduly optimistic and unwittingly sadistic teachers) to pin their hopes on careers they are unlikely to achieve. . . . About four hundred artists make a satisfactory living by touring throughout the country in solo recitals and concert performances. Public demand is not large enough to provide consistent work for more.*

Part of the difficulty lies in the great gap that still separates the professional from the amateur. Too much music teaching has been oriented toward training the potential virtuoso. Many a person who would have made an excellent amateur performer has been discouraged from music by the forced attempt to have him conquer the virtuoso's regime and his enormous repertoire, and too many students feel that if they cannot achieve this level, they cannot do anything at all worth while. They might be surprised and encouraged to learn how much great music was written specifically for amateurs of very limited attainments. There are valid ways of making music of the highest rank without arduous training.

The condition of even the successful professional is little better. As often as not, the performer in a symphony orchestra is a man hardened and embittered by the music business, who never touches his instrument in his free time if he can possibly help it.

The only development that might help would be the growth of widespread support of good musical activities at the community level, completely out of reach of concert bureaus. Groups such as small orchestras, chamber music ensembles, and choruses might afford a meeting ground for professionals and amateurs, fruitful for both.

If the professional performer is too often a hardened cynic, the amateur usually suffers from the defect that he can never subordinate himself to the task at hand sufficiently to do elementary justice to the music being studied. Performers know that the worst professional is usually better than the best amateur in that he knows how to work and put the music into decent shape.

* Cecil Smith, *Worlds of Music,* pp. 14-15 (Philadelphia and New York, 1952).

If community music could be encouraged, and this is a growing tendency, a healthy musical life might be restored.

We buy musical performances as we buy professional baseball games. But where, as Arthur Judson once asked, are the sandlot musical teams? Choruses, amateur and semi-professional orchestras, small opera companies, chamber music groups in homes and schools—these are the activities which build permanent identification with music in people who love the art because they have tried, however inadequately, to make music themselves. . . .

It is not too much to suggest that communities undertake to pay part of the cost of local music-making with public funds. The willingness of chambers of commerce and civic groups to purchase uniforms for marching bands and to help out with the cost of staging high-school operettas is a token of pride in the attainments of the local community. The aims of such civic enthusiasts need to be raised so that municipal or organized community support of orchestras, small opera companies, and other nonprofit musical enterprises may become the rule rather than the exception.

Not all musical performances require large expensive resources. A convincing program of education is needed to persuade the public, or the potential public, that chamber music groups, opera workshops, and small orchestras are able to provide music no less satisfying and beautiful than the music in the symphonic repertory or than the works played by visiting virtuosos. In this country good music is too largely equated with big or expensive music. . . . It costs very little to maintain a small chorus capable of singing expertly the madrigals of Morley or the motets of Brahms; within their scope these works are no less masterpieces than Bach's B minor Mass and the four Brahms symphonies. This is not to propose that small organizations take the place of larger ones; but the musical public needs to learn much more fully than it has the great delights of a vast literature that is relatively simple and inexpensive to perform.*

* *Worlds of Music,* pp. 171-172.

CHAPTER 9

Music as a Practical Craft

Creation

The composer creates specific forms out of the basic forms of music—melody, harmony, and rhythm. The growth and development of each unfolds at the same time. In all such creation one finds a contrast between the elements of consistency and variety in the composition, a variety of invention bound by consistency of style. In melody the element of consistency is represented by the tonal system adopted by the composer, the scale. In harmony it is represented by the cadences, and in rhythm by the meter. The element of variety is represented by the invention and imagination particular to a given composer, the particular shapes and forces that he discovers.

But a composer need not be particularly inventive or creative in order to be a composer, even a very prolific one. All that is needed is a repertoire of stock musical formulas; these constitute the craft of musical composition. It was only in some of the literary fantasies of the romantic era that the idea arose of composition as an outpouring of inspiration untouched by reflection or by considerations of practical limitations. Yet it would be a heavy task to create a composition of inspiration alone, without the aid of preexistent formulas and procedures. The craftsmen among composers did not have to wait upon inspiration, and indeed, the practical conditions under which they wrote left no time for such waiting. They were able to begin simply by manipulating standard formulas, like the improvisers of ancient music. If they happened to begin writing at a fortunate moment, the material took fire, but if not, they were at least able to turn out a respectable piece of work. And it was by no means a condition of their employment or of the existence of their music that it had to be artistically valuable; in most instances it sufficed merely if the music went well and did not intrude very much upon the practical occasion for which it was written. Only in exceptional cases, where a churchman or nobleman happened to be a lover or a connoisseur of music, did he go out of his way to employ a more gifted composer. A famous letter, frequently cited, may be mentioned again in this respect. The Grand Duke of Ferrara, Hercules, wished to employ a composer at his court in approximately the year 1500. His secretary wrote him that of two composers available, Heinrich Isaac and Josquin des Prez, he recommended engaging the former, because "Isaac is able to get on with his colleagues better and composes new pieces more quickly. . . . It is true that Josquin composes better, but only when it suits him and not when you want him to."

The idea that inspiration is something divorced from, or antagonistic to, the intellect and to the knowledge of musical material, is a romantic one, and the triumph of this idea has resulted in a serious decay in the craft of musical composition. Since the romantic era, technical mastery has become exceptional among composers, and much more difficult to achieve.

But it would be unjust to the romantic era to deny that it altered the general conception of the work of art, and at the same time came closer to understanding its significance. The romantic era first proclaimed the work of art as possessing a spiritual content—whatever may be understood by that—and therefore claimed for the artist a place more than ornamental in our civilization.

It was the one-sided emphasis upon the irrational which produced the deterioration of romantic music into the striving for effect, if no longer upon the mind and heart, at least upon the nerves.

However, for practical purposes the process of composition may be understood as the creation of movement in space and time, of motion from certain points toward particular goals, and the discovery or invention of particular shapes that embody that motion.

PERFORMANCE

The first musical instruments were undoubtedly human voices, hands, and feet. It is not difficult to imagine the origins of the different instruments. The archer's bow was the first stringed instrument; reeds were the first flutes; the first horns were probably animals' horns—rams' horns, elephants', and so on. The great horn of Roland was called Olivant (Elephant). The finest musical instrument of all remains the human voice. Its characteristics and limitations exert an influence upon our comprehension of music, upon the designs of musical instruments, and even upon the very techniques of composing.

Many features of singing in chorus, a practice as old as music, are recognizable in our purely orchestral music today. Thus, antiphonal writing, in which one group of voices answers another, or in which a group of voices imitates a soloist, and the repetition of melodies in high and low registers, are all traits in purely instrumental music reminiscent of choral singing.

The human voice has governed the design of musical intruments. The human voice divides into female, high and low (soprano and alto), and male, high and low (tenor and bass), with of course other intermediate ranges—contralto and baritone, which are less frequent. The first four comprise the great majority. For centuries the musical instruments of Europe were designed in families of varying size, in direct correspondence to the human chorus of soprano, alto, tenor, and bass. All these terms are applied to a larger or smaller version of some familiar instrument: we have the clarinet, and also the bass clarinet, the saxophone and the alto saxophone, the recorder, the tenor recorder, and so on.

Many of these instruments have fallen out of use; not every design of a musical instrument can create a satisfactory tone over a wide range of pitch. The family of instruments capable of most successfully maintaining a uniform, homogeneous texture of sound over a wide range is the violin family. The others are not comparably successful as ensembles. Due to gaps in their ranges, wind ensembles are rather heterogeneously composed: flutes, reeds, brasses. They do not blend so well together: some have much more piercing tone qualities, others do not speak with equal facility. A rapid melody, quite successful for a flute, may be impossible for a horn. The nucleus of ensemble music in general is, therefore, the string family, and the string quartet is the instrumental group which most successfully emulates the grouping of human voices in chorus.

Vocal music is traceable in the technique of composition; even the writing of instrumental parts is still called, correctly, *voice-leading*.

Mechanical instruments, such as music boxes, electronic devices, and instruments of stone or metal have very little use in our music. This is due to their being very far from having an "organic" character. The instruments most in use are those closest to the feel of an organism—everyone, by virtue of the use of his lungs and by the tensing of muscles, feels an instinctive kinship with winds and strings. Furthermore, that music which is most directly activated by a living organism speaks most closely to us. The more the action of an instrument is mediated by a mechanism, the more tiring it becomes. The most beautiful tone is that most immediately generated by the living organism.

Thus the mechanical reproduction of music, even when intensified to a high degree of accuracy, suffers from an inherent defect, the loss of immediacy. A live performance, even by amateurs, imperfect though it may be, is much more vivid and arresting than a good recording of a polished professional rendition.

THE VOICE AS AN INSTRUMENT

The development of instrumental music since the seventeenth century has led to an enormous extension of vocal technique. Whereas the vocal music of the Renaissance, and also most choral music since then, was written for untrained voices, a large body of vocal music appeared which can be performed only by trained voices, voices which have been forced to rival instruments. The extension of voice technique reached its apparent limits in the field of opera, whose music requires long and arduous training. Wagner expected a single human voice to make itself heard over a large symphony orchestra at its loudest and the composers of Italian opera made the voice a rival of flutes and violins in range and agility.

Special training of the voice evolved. But the human voice is a mysterious instrument; it is difficult to investigate its acoustical functioning.

There are in existence many schools and methods of vocal training, many of which claim an exclusive scientific basis. Because of the impossibility of investigating the mechanics of singing as easily as those of instruments, their scientific status is not certain, although specific teachers are known to gain consistently good results. Vocal training is highly subjective in language. The instructions of voice teachers, to "shape" a tone, or to "project the tone across the room," and so on, have no objective meaning, but are intended to bring about a certain setting and relaxation of the very complex system used in singing—the lungs and diaphragm, the throat and larynx, and the lips, tongue, and jaw. About the only points on which the many conflicting voice methods seem to be in agreement are the extension of breath control, the relaxational enlargement of the throat, and the elimination of unnecessary muscular tensions. Nevertheless the field remains a confusion of conflicting claims and procedures.

MUSICAL INSTRUMENTS

For practical purposes instruments may be divided into the following classes: strings, winds, keyboard instruments, drums and bells, and miscellaneous.

STRINGED INSTRUMENTS

Stringed instruments are those in which the sound is generated by a vibrating string. Any string vibrating by itself produces a very feeble sound and therefore some amplification is necessary. In the violin and the guitar, a sound-chest is formed by the body of the instrument and by the air it contains. In those keyboard instruments which are stringed, such a sound-chest is formed by the sounding board and the air contained inside the instrument. Strings may be activated by a bow, a hammer, or plucked either by the finger or by a mechanical device.

The string instruments sounded by a bow are those of the violin family.

The Violin Family

The instruments of the violin family went through many experiments and evolutions before reaching their present forms. Some evidence of these many essays survives in the names for these instruments. The Italian word *violino* is a diminutive, meaning small viol (the *viols* were the ancestors of the violin family). The word *violoncello* is a strange hybrid. The *violone* was a large viol, the suffix *cello* is a diminutive, and the violoncello is a smaller version of the large viol. Even today the double bass is also called the bass viol.

The string family is normally grouped as a quartet: two violins, viola, and violoncello. The string section of the orchestra is a multiplication of this arrangement, supplemented by a double bass section. The double bass is hardly used outside of large orchestras, and almost never in chamber music.

Although the literature for string quartet is the finest available for any single category of music, the violin family is not only the medium of great art. The instruments themselves are artistic creations of a very high order.

The Plucked Instruments

Of these there are two main groups: first the lute, guitars, and mandolins, and secondly, harps and lyres. The instruments in the first category are structurally related to violins in that they all possess a sound chest, strings stretched over a bridge, and a fingerboard on which the player obtains notes of different pitch from each string by shortening or lengthening the vibrating length of the string. The violin's design is, in fact, a descendant of the lute's.

Harps and lyres are conditioned by having each string set to a definite pitch and to that pitch only, in contrast to such instruments as violins and guitars.

The Lute. The lute in the sixteenth and seventeenth centuries held a position comparable to that of the piano in the last half of the nineteenth century and the first part of the twentieth; it was of enormous popularity, to be found in countless homes. It passed into eclipse in the eighteenth century, partly due to the rise of the harpsichord, which assumed its functions in instrumental music, and partly to that of the guitar, which replaced it in accompanying the voice. A very large literature of music, composed for the lute as well as arranged for it, survives, indicating the importance it once held. Because of this music the lute has been revived in our own time. It came to Europe from the Near East; the Arabic name is *al ūd,* from which the European name is derived. In the Near East it has never fallen out of use.

The Guitars. The Spanish and Italian guitars eclipsed the lute in the eighteenth and nineteenth centuries and there is a large body of music written specifically for these instruments. The widespread interest in the guitar among amateurs helped bring about simplification of its design to the present form.

The Mandolin. This is another outgrowth of the lute and guitar forms, and a popular folk instrument. Mozart wrote for the instrument in his *Don Giovanni*, and Verdi in his *Otello*.

The Harps and Lyres. These instruments dominated the music of the Celts, as well as that of Greece, but are extinct today. The harp survives in modern use in the orchestra, mostly as a supporting instrument. The body of music in which the harp plays an important part is not large.

The modern harp is tuned to the major scale in C-flat. It has been equipped with pedals for adjusting the pitches chromatically. With one pedal all the C strings can be changed from C-flat to C-natural or to C-sharp. With the next pedal, the same is done for the D strings, and so on. There are seven pedals, one for each tone of the scale. It should be realized that when the pedal mechanism is used, all of the strings producing the tone governed by that pedal are altered in pitch. The setting of the harp is somewhat cumbersome, which rather restricts its versatility. Its use in orchestral music has been mostly for the elaboration of certain harmonic formulas; the harp can be set to sound a few chords and to play them rapidly and sonorously. This has been its chief use.

The relative decline of the plucked instruments as compared to the violins is due to the triumph of instrumental music over vocal music. The plucked instruments cannot produce a sustained tone, only a short, sharp, detached sound, which fades out rapidly. Such a tone is ideally suited to accompanying a singer, especially the singer who wishes to accompany himself. It is not well suited to the polyphonic style which the violin family serves so well. Plucked instruments—the lute and the classical guitar—have been revived today, and have never fallen out of use in vocal music. In addition to the large literature already existing for these instruments, a new literature for them is being produced today.

WIND INSTRUMENTS

The column of air contained inside a pipe may act as a vibrating body. The normal pressure of the atmosphere tends to keep the air in the pipe at a stable density, but it is subject to impulses toward compression and rarefaction. The rapid alternation of the density of the air about its norm produces audible vibrations. Although we distinguish in our terminology between "woodwinds" and "brasses," the materials of which the pipe is made play almost no part in determining its sound quality. The brassy timbre of the trumpet is not a result of the brass of which it is made, but of the shape of its bore, the flare of the bell, and the way the trumpeter's lips set the air in vibration: these all combine to produce overtones of high frequency that add brilliance to the tone. Pipes made of wood and properly designed can produce the same timbre, and similarly, there are woodwinds made of metal whose timbres are no less that of the woodwinds.

The column of air inside a pipe may be set into vibration in several ways: (1) By an "edge tone." In the recorder, flute, the flue-pipes of the organ, and even the common penny whistle, a stream of air is directed against a sharp edge and is thereby split into a series of rapid eddies or whorls on either side of the edge; these in turn set the body of air inside the pipe into action. (2) By reeds. In the clarinets and saxophones, the player blows at one end of the pipe into a mouthpiece to which a reed is attached. The vibrations of the reed act as a valve, opening and closing the end of the pipe. The puffs of air which are thus rapidly and continuously introduced into the pipe set the column of air into vibration. In the oboes and bassoons, the activating agent is a double reed. (3) In the brass instruments, the trumpets, trombones, and horns, it is the player's lips set into the mouthpiece that play the part of vibrating reeds.

The pitch of a pipe may be altered in three ways, by shortening it, by lengthening it, and by overblowing. If a hole is opened in the side of the pipe, the air beyond the hole escapes the vibrating impulses, and the effective length of the pipe is shortened, the body of air is diminished, and a higher pitch is produced. Holes may be systematically arranged in the pipe to produce a complete scale, as in all the woodwinds. The effective vibrating length of a pipe may be increased by attaching to it some extra lengths of tubing that are closed off until some valve is opened. When the valve is opened, the increased mass of air will vibrate at a lower frequency and produce a tone of lower pitch. This is the function performed by the various systems of valves and tubing to be seen in the trumpets, horns, and tubas. In the trombone, the vibrating length is increased simply by moving out the slide.

The tone generated by a length of pipe may be altered by overblowing. By proper setting of his lips and by increased force of blowing, the player may cause the tone to jump to one or another higher overtone. The woodwind instruments are somewhat cumbersome in this respect, and only the first two or three overtones are used. The brass instruments are very agile and can sound a large number of the higher overtones; these are their principal notes. Everyone is familiar with the ease with which the bugle shifts from one overtone to another; these are, in fact, the only tones available to it.

The pipe described so far is somewhat abstract and idealized. What has been said is true as long as the pipe is a simple column of air. But in practice there are a number of complicating and distorting factors. The pipe for the column of air may be bent and twisted into various shapes for convenience in carrying, as we see in the trumpets, horns, trombones, and tubas. Furthermore, the column of air may be a simple cylinder, as in organ pipes, the flute, and clarinet. It may also be a cone—as in the oboes—or a complicated mixture of the two—as in the trumpets—which are partially conical and partially cylindrical at different parts of the bore. The bending of the air column and the shapes of the bore exert an influence upon the tonal qualities of wind instruments, and consequently upon the techniques of playing them. The bending of the air column tends to distort the pitch of the overtones, pulling them out of tune to a certain extent. The instruments are designed to keep the distortions within certain limits for most of the range of the instrument, and the player of a brass instrument can, by setting his lips, adjust the pitch toward the true overtone. But the intonation of brass instruments is proverbially weak. The shape of the bore tends to suppress or reinforce certain overtones. A cylindrical pipe such as the clarinet has no even-numbered overtones; when the clarinetist overblows, the instrument jumps up to the third partial as the second is not available. Instruments of conical bore such as the oboe, have the even-numbered partials.

Achieving a Scale

The complex mechanisms of wind instruments were developed in response to the wish to have complete scales available to composers. A pipe normally makes available just its fundamental tone and some of its overtones, and the only variety of pitch is that available by skipping from one overtone to another. The gaps have to be filled in to create a complete scale. The solution applied by the brass instruments is simply to make more air available, and thereby lower the pitch of the fundamental by successive steps, thus filling in the gaps. In the woodwinds, the gap is filled in the opposite direction. By shortening the pipe, the pitch is successively raised until the next overtone is reached; then, by closing the holes and so returning the pipe to its full length, and overblowing, the process is repeated in the higher register of the instrument.

The many refinements in the mechanisms and shaping of wind instruments have altered their characteristics over the years and the gains in range and facility have been paid for with a loss of tonal quality and power. Bach and Mozart might be astonished to hear modern oboes, clarinets, and horns, and there is some reason to believe that our modern instruments may not be fully appropriate to orchestration as they intended it.

Furthermore, these developments have been such as to render the fundamental tones unavailable. What we call the clarinet in B-flat may once have had B-flat as its fundamental and may even have been able to sound it, but such a time is long past if not mythological. Hardly any brass instrument can play the fundamental on which it is said to be based, but the anachronism of referring to instruments as horns "in F," or trumpets "in B-flat," and so on, persists.

The manufacture and playing of wind instruments is mostly a practical craft. Scientific theory is surprisingly undeveloped in this field, and indeed is still under way. It has given rise to a few developments but is mostly devoted to explaining how the instruments accomplish what they do. The manufacture of each instrument still involves a large amount of trial and error, and brass instruments made by different manufacturers differ in their measurements to a surprising extent, even though they sound very much the same. Their complexities have not permitted them to create ensembles with the homogeneity and agility of the stringed instruments, and they have been traditionally much more instruments of solo and of contrast than have the string sections.

The Flutes

The modern flute is a pipe stopped at one end. The mouthpiece is in the side of the instrument, near one end. The tone is produced by a stream of air directed by the player's lips against the sharp edge of the mouthpiece; the stream of air is set into vibration and in turn activates the air inside the pipe. It is an instrument of relatively recent date. The old transverse flutes were not much in evidence before the sixteenth century; their form underwent a series of mechanical innovations, the most important of which is the Boehm mechanism of the nineteenth century that gives the instrument great range and facility. Flutes displaced recorders after the eighteenth century.

The Piccolo

The full name of the piccolo is *flauto piccolo,* small flute. It sounds an octave higher than written.

There is also a larger flute, the bass flute.

The Recorders

These were the flutes of earlier music. Their tone is activated by the simple mouthpiece of the penny whistle. The stream of air is directed against the sharp beveled edge of the mouthpiece and so set in vibration. The recorder family consists of soprano, alto, tenor, bass, and contrabass, and also a very small *sopranino*. The recorder, like the harpsichord and the guitar, has experienced a revival today, and may even become the principal instrument of amateur music making.

The Oboes

The oboes are double reed instruments, descendants of the medieval schalmeys and pommers. The other instruments of this group are the *oboe d'amore* and the English horn.

The Bassoons

In their medieval forms, as bass pommers, these were the bass instruments of the oboe family; they are still double reed instruments but of entirely different tone quality.

Both oboes and bassoons have a long ancestry. Their modern forms are considerably changed, and consequently they no longer possess the tone color or power of their older forms. The double reeds, accordingly, do not produce a coherent quality of tone comparable to the violin family.

The Clarinets

The clarinet family is fairly large, there being eight members. Of these the clarinets in C, D, and E-flat are obsolescent, and the alto clarinet and basset horn are rare, and only the clarinets in B-flat and A are in common use.

BRASS INSTRUMENTS

The first horns were animal horns and served not for musical purposes but as signals. The earliest musical horns were direct imitations of the animal horn shapes, and indeed produced sounds much more like noise than like tone. From the hunting horn evolved the modern orchestral horn, the French horn, and from military trumpets and bugles the orchestral valve trumpets developed, and from the postillion horn came the modern cornet.

The very confusion and diversity of designs among the brass instruments indicates their more peripheral position with respect to art music. These instruments have never received the refinement and standardization of design to be found among string, woodwind, and keyboard instruments. Most of our orchestras attempt to make do with a few of the most common brass instruments, rather than keep on hand the immense variety of brass instruments which have been called for in orchestral literature from time to time. Much of the difficulty involved in performing older music accurately stems from the difference between the sound of the modern standard instruments and their older and more powerful forms.

The Trumpets

With crooks, the pitch of a trumpet can be lowered: it can be a trumpet in C, B-flat, or A.

The Bass Trumpet

This was originally designed by Wagner to fill out the range of the trumpets, but the design turned out to be not fully practical, and the instrument is not widely used.

The Cornet

This is not a trumpet, but is derived from the post horn. It is more facile in character than the trumpet; it is usually tuned to B-flat or A.

The French Horns

These are the most beautiful of the brass instruments, with an important literature of concertos and chamber music. They are usually in F.

The Trombones

There are alto, tenor, bass, and double bass trombones. In practice, the tenor (B-flat) and bass (in G) are used, the others rarely.

The Tubas

The euphonium, E-flat bass, B-flat bass, and Wagnerian tubas are really modified horns. The true tubas are wide-bore instruments in which it is possible to reach and sound the fundamental tones. Modern narrow-bore instruments, our trumpets and horns, cannot do this. Out of the Wagnerian instruments grew a whole series of hybrids sharing traits of both tubas and horns, among them the saxhorns and sousaphones.

The Saxophones

These, like the saxhorns, are named for their inventor, Adolphe Sax. They are hybrid instruments. As in the oboe and bassoon, they are of conical bore; as in the clarinets they are sounded by a single reed; and as in the trumpets, they are made of brass. The family contains seven members, but in practice the alto, tenor, and baritone saxophones are most commonly used. These are among the last truly new musical instruments to have been invented. It should be remarked that the saxophone had a fifty-year history in the symphony orchestra, mostly in France, before it became the staple jazz instrument.

KEYBOARD INSTRUMENTS

The keyboard instruments of today are the organ, the harpsichord, the clavichord, and the piano. The organ is the oldest, and was known among the Greeks. Until the Middle Ages it was operated by a series of slides which were pulled in and out. The keyboard itself was invented in the thirteenth century and made the playing of the organ a much less ponderous operation. Organ building and playing increased greatly after this time.

The keyboard was as promptly applied to the activation of strings and the result was the clavichord. The clavichord appears to have been an outgrowth of the old monochord, and for a time instruments having many strings were still referred to as monochords. The harpsichord and piano were later developments.

The Well-Tempered Keyboard

The player of a wind or string instrument is free to alter the pitch of almost any note he sounds. If a violinist should play a note slightly out of tune, he may swiftly adjust the pitch by moving his finger along the string; the wind player whose intonation is insecure may adjust the pitch by slight variations in the air pressure and in the setting of his lips. But the players of keyboard instruments are confronted with a mechanism that mediates between them and the sound, and they are unable to adjust the pitch of individual notes once their instruments have been tuned.

This rigidity of tuning has posed serious problems to composers and performers of keyboard music. It happens that not one tone in our music has a definite pitch which is correct for it under all musical circumstances. The pitch of a tone shifts according to its relations with other tones. Thus, the E that is a fifth above A has a slightly different pitch from the E that is a third above C. Different intervals conflict and cause tones to shift in pitch. The conflict is due to the fact that we can derive the tone E in more than one way. We may start from C and create tones by successive fifths: from C to G, G to D, D to A, and finally A to E. Each string in the series is 2/3 the length of the preceding string, so that the value corresponding to E is 16/81 of the original string length. But the E that is the overtone of C has the value 1/5, or 16/80. The slight difference between the two values is called a *comma.*

It happens that every tone is not fixed, but variable, according to how it is derived; there is no limit to the number of commas. It is mostly a matter of harmony that determines which is just the right pitch for a tone in the course of a composition. Players of keyboard instruments cannot adjust the pitch of tones as they go along, as can players of strings and winds, and as singers can, and this rigidity of intonation has caused all the problems for tuning keyboard instruments. The earlier systems, the Pythagorean and just intonations, gave keyboards pure and beautiful sounds within some keys, but made it impossible to play in others.

The tuning system in effect today is called *even temperament.* It won decisive acceptance over the others in Bach's lifetime; in fact, Bach's forty-eight preludes and fugues, *The Well-Tempered Keyboard,* were written in all keys to show the one decisive advantage of this system over the others, namely, that one can play equally well in all keys without retuning. This is essential for a musical art in which modulation, the shift from one key to another, plays a fundamental part. Even temperament is a system of deliberate mistuning in which every interval but the octave is falsified, but only slightly, as against the older systems in which some intervals were quite pure and others completely distorted. In even temperament, the octave is filled with twelve equal steps, none of which forms a true interval with any other, but is close enough. Thus, the fourth tone of this system is neither D-sharp nor E-flat, but close enough to serve as either in the appropriate context. Similarly, the eighth tone is not truly G, but is close enough to pass for it.

The result of these compromises is that the keyboard instruments are always slightly impure and slightly out of tune. In order to have keyboards capable of playing with as accurate intonation as other instruments, up to fifty keys would be needed to the octave, instead of the twelve now employed. Fortunately, the mind and ear are able to recognize true relations through imperfect realizations of them. Recent experiments with even temperament indicate that it may be capable of great improvement without complicating the keyboard structure.

The Organ

The organ is a wind instrument; the keyboard activates a row of pipes that are on a wind chest. There is in the wind chest a constant supply of compressed air that is maintained at a steady pressure. Depressing a key opens a valve to its corresponding pipe, and the compressed air is set in vibration inside the pipe. A simple organ will consist of one set of pipes; each such set is termed a stop. Because pipes can be made to sound a great variety of tone colors, most organs are equipped with many stops. Those of Bach's time ranged from about one to three dozen stops, each of different volume and timbre.

It is common for most organs to have two and more keyboards or manuals, each with its own sets of stops and timbres, and also to have a pedal. The pedal is essentially an enlarged keyboard operated by the feet and it extends the range of the organ below that of the manuals.

The organ pipes are of two kinds, the flue pipes and the reeds. To the flue pipes belong those stops called principal and diapason; these generate the tones we think of as proper to the organ itself. Others are labeled "flute" and "string" tones and, because of the partial tones they generate, are able to imitate these instruments quite vividly.

The reed pipes include those stops labeled "trumpets," "trombones," "posaunes," and others, and once again are remarkably evocative of brass and woodwind instruments.

A very large number of organ pipes, each of different size and shape, may be built to a given pitch; each will have its own tone color, and many will serve to imitate other instruments with great vividness. There are more than twenty such designs possible.

Since every era has modified or enlarged the organ to suit its musical interests, it is hard to speak of the organ as a single instrument; it is just as much a conglomerate of instruments. The multiple keyboards themselves testify to this; they represent an amalgam into one instrument of organs which were once in different parts of a cathedral. The nineteenth century witnessed an enormous expansion of the organ in an effort to make it a rival to the symphony orchestra, and there have existed huge mechanisms with hundreds of stops and as many as seven keyboards. All this was made possible partly by the great versatility of pipes in imitating all kinds of timbres, and by the substitution of the electric motor for the hand labor of pumping air. In order for Bach to play the organ the labor of a few apprentices, pumping long and hard at the bellows, was required. The use of electricity and of a host of new mechanical and electrical devices made possible the development of the organ to an enormity.

The organ of the Baroque era, during which the greatest literature for the instrument was created, was much lighter and more modest. The composer Michael Praetorius published complete details for building an organ in his *Syntagma Musicum* in the early part of the seventeenth century. This, and the organs of the great instrument maker Silbermann, who was contemporary with Bach, have been carefully emulated by some modern organ builders. The result has been to restore the organ to its place as one of the noblest and most beautiful of instruments.

Along with the beauty of the organ must be mentioned its handicap, the inability to differentiate tones by volume. Because the wind pressure is even, the organist cannot emphasize a desired tone or sequence of tones by increasing its volume. As simultaneous melodies are not easily distinguished, the organ is ill suited for the performance of polyphonic music. Nevertheless, its history and its position in sacred music have made it a polyphonic instrument.

The Clavichord

Each string of the clavichord is set in vibration by a metal tangent that not only serves to sound it, but cuts off its vibrating length, and therefore determines the pitch. It is the oldest of the stringed keyboard instruments, going at least as far back as the thirteenth century. Of all the musical instruments, it has the softest and most delicate tone, and can hardly be heard at all beyond the limits of a small room. It is related by Bach's first biographer, Forkel, that

> he liked best to play upon the clavichord; the harpsichord, though certainly susceptible of a great variety of expression, had not soul enough for him; and the piano was in his lifetime too much in its infancy and still much too coarse to satisfy him.*

* Hans David and Arthur Mendel, *The Bach Reader*, p. 311 (New York, 1945).

The Harpsichord

The strings of the harpsichord are plucked by a series of sliding jacks. Because of the mode of operation of its mechanism, all the tones of its keyboard are of the same degree of loudness. Many harpsichords were built with two manuals, one loud and one soft. From the sixteenth century to the eighteenth, it was the foremost keyboard instrument for secular music; it suffered its total eclipse by the piano only when the latter instrument was perfected toward the end of the eighteenth century. The literature for the harpsichord, as for its earlier relative, the virginal, is large and valuable. The harpsichord, like the Baroque organ, has seen a significant revival in our own day.

The Piano

This is the instrument of Western music which is perhaps the most popular and most widespread of all. It caused the clavichord and harpsichord to be all but forgotten, overshadowed the organ, and created an entire epoch in music making, even into our own day. It is possibly the most difficult of all instruments to master. Its outstanding characteristic is its great flexibility, in contrast to the organ, harpsichord, and clavichord. As its full name *piano e forte* implies, it was the first keyboard instrument on which it was possible to play all possible gradations of loudness and softness with one keyboard. (Of course, the clavichord is capable of gradations of volume, but the clavichord at its loudest is very soft indeed.)

The ancestor of the piano appears to have been the dulcimer, a stringed instrument struck with hammers. Many attempts were made to evolve a suitable hammer mechanism, but it was not until 1709 that such a mechanism was perfected by Bartolomeo Cristofori. This may be said to mark the birth of the true piano. Bach was greatly interested in the development of the piano, as we observed before, but found the early attempts by Silbermann unsatisfactory.

He had praised, indeed admired, its tone; but he had complained that it was too weak in the high register, and was too hard to play. This had been taken greatly amiss by Mr. Silbermann, who could not bear to have any fault found in his handiworks. He was therefore angry at Mr. Bach for a long time. And yet his conscience told him that Mr. Bach was not wrong. He therefore decided . . . to think all the harder about how to eliminate the faults Mr. J. S. Bach had observed. He worked for many years on this. . . . Finally, when Mr. Silbermann had really achieved many improvements, notably in respect to the action, . . . [he] had the laudable ambition to show one of these instruments of his later workmanship to the late Kapellmeister Bach, and have it examined by him; and he had received, in turn, complete approval from him.*

It may not, then, be sacrilege to play Bach's music on the piano.

The piano, like most other instruments, went through a long and complex series of technical improvements and transformations before reaching the position of giant of the nineteenth century concert hall. Some of its intermediate stages are historically important. The type of piano favored by Mozart, and even later by Chopin, was one of lighter weight and caliber than the later instruments. It was Beethoven who rejoiced in the larger and more rugged English instrument by Broadwood and who gave decisive impetus to the continued development of the piano.

The piano was the instrument of musical romanticism. Its evanescent tone, which slowly fades but suggests its presence even after it has faded, makes it, more than any other instrument, a device for suggesting and creating musical illusions. This has the defect of blurring musical relations; on the piano, dissonances are less sharp, and consonances less clear. But its very suggestiveness, and the richness of its tones, make it an instrument of great versatility. There is hardly any music in the literature that cannot be arranged satisfactorily for and performed at the piano by four hands, if not by two, making the instrument one of almost universal scope. It is only when used in conjunction with the violin family that its limitations are painfully evident. Then the percussive element in piano tone, as well as its evocation of the illusion rather than the reality of a sustained singing tone, are shown up.

* Quotation from Johann Friedrich Agricola in *The Bach Reader*, p. 259.

Other Keyboard Instruments

The keyboard serves a few other instruments. The celesta is a set of chimes activated by a piano mechanism, and there is also a glockenspiel with keyboard attachment. Some carillons (the bells in church towers) are also operated from keyboards.

THE PERCUSSION INSTRUMENTS

Those of Definite Pitch

The most important of the tuned percussion instruments are the kettledrums. These are equipped with devices about the rim for tightening and loosening the membranes, and so acquiring a definite pitch. They occur normally in pairs, a large and a small drum, though intermediate sizes exist. Hardly a classic symphony has been written without employing them. They were indispensable to Beethoven, who greatly extended the range of tunings for them.

Church bells structurally are metal plates that are fixed in the center and that vibrate freely about the edges. The bent shape into which they are cast distorts the partial vibrations and results in the characteristically muddy tone of the bells. Because of their great size and weight, they have never been used in concert music but many composers have wished to imitate the sound of church bells in their compositions. The orchestral bells used for this purpose are tubular steel bars.

The glockenspiel consists of a set of small steel plates arranged in a frame and struck with hammers. There was an older keyboard glockenspiel, now somewhat rare, for which Mozart wrote in his *Magic Flute*. It originated as a toy imitation of church carillons but the bells have been replaced by steel plates. The celesta is a more recent form of the keyboard glockenspiel in which the tone is improved by wooden resonators. It looks very much like an upright piano, and in fact uses a modified piano mechanism.

The xylophone is constructed of sticks of hard wood of sufficient resonance to produce specific tones. It is an instrument of great antiquity, widely used throughout the world, and a popular folk instrument. Its most famous use in the symphony orchestra is in Saint-Saën's *Danse Macabre*. Many other composers, most notably Mahler, have made use of it.

Percussion Instruments of No Definite Pitch

The Drums. All drums consist of membranes stretched over a frame, enclosing a body of air to add resonance and force to the noise. It is interesting to note that the human voice has lent its name even to instruments of no definite pitch, the tenor and bass drums. Both of these, especially the bass drum, have played an important role in symphonic literature. The snare drum features a bundle of taut strings stretched across the lower drumhead, producing the characteristic noise of this instrument.

Other instruments without definite pitch which have played parts in our music are tambourines, triangles, cymbals, gongs, and castanets.

FOLK INSTRUMENTS

There are a host of instruments in use throughout the world that have not found their way into our art music, except for occasional experiments. Among them are zithers, hurdy-gurdies, banjos, ukuleles, ocarinas, and many others. The instruments of our concert life, described above, are derivatives of folk instruments, shaped for artistic purposes. The orchestral horn is the sophisticated cousin of the hunting horn which continues in use, the violin is the descendant of primitive fiddles, the trumpet of old military instruments.

Folk instruments remain a respository for composers seeking new stylistic resources. Many a composer has turned to these instruments, and simply by writing for one of them has brought it into the orchestral circle.

Also to be found among folk instruments are those which were once important for art music but have since fallen into neglect; the lute and the Irish harp are among them.

ENSEMBLE MUSIC

Music has been written for all kinds of architectural conditions, both in- and out-of-doors. There are sonatas to be played from church towers, music for processions, sonatas for church (*da chiesa*) and for private rooms (*da camera*), and of course there is music for large public halls—the opera theater and the symphony hall. Ensemble music has been influenced not merely by the logic of grouping instruments, but by architectural considerations.

Chamber Music

Chamber music generally means any music for small ensembles, music of an intimate character and therefore appropriate to small rooms. Originally intended for the private salons of the nobility, today it is often performed in large concert halls. It is not generally taken to include vocal music, though the large repertoire of *lieder* since Schubert is more appropriate to the small room than to the concert hall. There is also a large amount of *hausmusik*, written specifically for the home. This is generally taken to mean chamber music of easier character—much chamber music proper being extremely difficult—and does include music for voice.

The style of writing for chamber music generally exhibits greater attention to nuance and detail, much of which would be lost in the orchestra. There are some compositions for chamber ensembles written in an orchestral or concerto style which seem like an intrusion into chamber music; some of them are, however, redeemed by their musical interest.

The most important ensemble for chamber music is the string quartet—two violins, viola, and violoncello. This group is frequently augmented by another instrument—piano, another viola or cello, or even a wind instrument—to form a quintet. Duos, trios, sextets, and so on also appear occasionally, but in most cases the essential makeup is strings, with or without a keyboard instrument. The standard labels for these groups are sometimes misleading; for instance a piano trio is not three pianos but piano, violin, and cello, and a clarinet quintet ordinarily is made up of a clarinet and a string quartet. The music written for any of these combinations is a variety of the instrumental sonata, just as the symphony is a sonata for orchestra. There is a first-rate literature for wind instruments alone, but compared to the volume of music for strings it is slight. Chamber music, especially that for string quartet, perhaps represents the highest achievement of all our music.

The Orchestra

The term *orchestra* comes from the Greek and originally meant the place in front of the Greek stage upon which the chorus sang and danced. When the opera was created in Italy, toward the end of the sixteenth century, with the intention of reviving Greek drama, the word was used for the place in front of the stage where the instruments accompanying the singers were located, and finally became applied to the instrumental ensemble itself.

Today we do not always think of the orchestra as having a connection with the theater. The composition of the orchestra has varied; the small orchestra of the classic composers, Haydn, Mozart, and the earlier Beethoven consisted primarily of the string group—first and second violins, violas, cellos, and basses—and a small number of wind instruments—two flutes, two oboes, two clarinets, two bassoons, two trumpets and two horns. There were also usually two kettledrums. The wind instruments were for contrast; the string section was mostly the core. Bach and Handel favored oboes, bassoons, and trumpets in their orchestras, much more than did the composers of the classic period. The clarinet came into the orchestra relatively late, and a number of symphonies by Haydn and Mozart were written without using it. Mozart in his later symphonies, especially the one in E-flat, made the clarinet an indispensable part of the orchestra. The orchestra of the later Beethoven and consequently of the romantic symphonists—Schumann, Brahms, Mendelssohn, and others—was expanded somewhat by the addition of trombones, more horns, and sometimes a wider range of percussion instruments.

Wagner expanded the orchestra greatly, especially in the brass section, and even went so far as to require new instruments—the so-called Wagner tubas—to fill out the range of brass instruments. The orchestra of the late romantic period sought more varied and more exotic tone colors, and the less customary forms of instruments —English horns, basset horns, bass clarinets, and so on—were explored.

The extreme limits of the orchestra were reached in the experiments of Berlioz and in some of the works of Mahler, in which the number of performers reached several hundred.

Orchestras have also existed according to types of instrument; much music has been written for string orchestra and for wind ensembles. Such groups lack the relief of contrast. Wind and brass ensembles have been favored for use out-of-doors because of their carrying power, brass instruments for military bands, woodwinds for serenades.

The growth and complexity of the modern orchestra has led to the rise of certain crafts, those of the orchestrator and conductor. Orchestration is something conceived of as separate from composition for orchestra; often a composer will write his composition first and then orchestrate it. In popular commercial music, a composer will write a melody and then turn it over to a professional arranger who adds accompaniment in various forms. The art of orchestrating is primarily a matter of knowing how instruments blend and combine; this is something akin to theatrical makeup, and many a poor musical idea has been covered over by clever orchestration.

THE CONDUCTOR

Conducting is very old; the ancient singers of chant were led by a method of direction called *cheironomy,* the term being derived from the Greek for shaping of the hand. The performers shaped their hands to recall the contours of the melody. Such direction can be seen on murals from Egypt. Conductors normally were performing members of their ensembles. In the Baroque orchestra, the keyboard player held this function and as the keyboard declined in the orchestra with the decline of figured bass, the first violinist assumed the director's functions. He is still called the concertmaster, and still performs an important function in carrying out the conductor's wishes. Conducting as a special métier was not definitely established until the nineteenth century, Felix Mendelssohn being the first concert conductor. He was also an accomplished performer, though many of the legion of professional conductors who followed him were not.

There are orchestras which have performed without conductors, and it is a commonplace joke among orchestral players that many orchestras perform *despite* their conductors. But this depends upon an ensemble of experienced performers. Conducting is a genuine skill, though an overrated one. The complexity of the orchestra and the many ways it is possible to perform a specific composition do call for some homogeneous method of performing, which can only be supplied by a director cooperating with his players. The virtuoso conductor, who is far removed from the practical skills of performing and who imposes his conceptions on the music, the players, and the audience, is an oppressive creation of the concert industry.

MUSICAL ARCHITECTURE

Many a hall built for musical purposes has turned out to be useless because of its poor acoustical properties. The science of building rooms to have good acoustical properties was neglected for centuries, although the ancients seem to have known much about it. Such Greek amphitheaters as survive today are unsurpassed for their acoustical excellence. Some of the ancients' theories of acoustical architecture come down to us. They maintained that the key not only to the acoustical properties of buildings but also their beauty was the use of harmonic proportions in the measuring of the rooms. The Roman architect Vitruvius remarked that all architects should be musically trained. The use of harmonic ratios in architecture has had a long history, but after the Renaissance architect Leon Battista Alberti, the practice has more or less died out. Only a few rules of thumb seem to have guided architects thereafter, and the acoustical property of rooms appears to have become a matter of chance.

The modern science of architectural acoustics was developed in the late nineteenth and early twentieth centuries, mostly by Professor Wallace C. Sabine of Harvard and his son, who began to investigate the problems when an auditorium newly built at Harvard turned out to be useless because of its reverberations. Their studies dealt mostly with the reflection and absorption of sound and with the shape of auditoriums.

The art of architectural acoustics is mainly one of avoiding an excess either of echoes or of dead spots in an auditorium, and of compensating for defects by the use of sound-absorbing or -reflecting materials. Their work was largely ignored until taken up by the radio and phonograph industries, for which acoustically good studios are essential. They also recognized the importance of the shape of rooms in focusing or deadening sounds and made specific recommendations for avoiding various geometric shapes. The power of the shape of a room to affect its acoustical properties is shown in such rooms as the Whispering Gallery in St. Paul's Cathedral in London, where a slight sound made at certain points beneath the dome is clearly heard directly opposite, but may be barely heard at intervening points. The best rooms, for acoustical purposes, are those that do not focus the sound in certain parts of the room, as in the Whispering Gallery, at the expense of others.

The modern science of acoustical architecture remains entirely empirical, and architects are not sure of the acoustical properties of the rooms they design until working models have been built and tested.

THE RECORDING AND REPRODUCTION OF MUSIC

THE PHONOGRAPH

The phonograph record is a disc which has been etched by a needle according to the vibrations to be recorded. From this record a master die of metal is made, and from the master, thousands of copies are imprinted on a plastic substance. When a record is played, the irregularities of its surface are transformed by a tracking needle into mechanical vibrations. The mechanical vibrations of the needle are converted into fluctuating electrical currents by the cartridge, which is normally either a magnetic device or a crystal which, when subject to varying pressures, emits varying electrical impulses. The electrical impulses are then amplified (magnified in power) by a series of electronic tubes in order that they may drive loudspeakers, which in their turn transform the varying electrical impulses into mechanical vibrations of the air. Thus a semblance of the original sounds are reproduced.

The earliest technical difficulties involved the narrow range of frequencies that could be successfully reproduced; this range has been steadily widened to the full range of audibility. Other difficulties concerned the loudspeakers; since small objects cannot easily generate low frequencies, and conversely, large objects do not easily generate high frequencies, loudspeakers were usually unable to respond accurately over the full range. Multiple loudspeakers have been devised, each to generate its most congenial range of frequencies, along with electronic instruments to send to each speaker its appropriate set of frequencies. Other difficulties have been similar to those faced by the builders of sounding boards in pianos and other instruments, namely that sounding boards or loudspeakers were required that responded ideally to as wide a range of vibrations as possible, not favoring by natural resonance, any one set of frequencies. Other problems have resulted from the distortions that loudspeakers and amplifiers offer at differing levels of sound, and the necessity of eliminating the slight surface irregularities of records which produce background scratches and hisses. (The principles of recording on film or on tape are fundamentally no different from those involved in plastic records; on film, the fluctuating vibrations are converted into fluctuations of light and dark, recorded on film emulsions, and on tape, into fluctuating degrees of magnetization of the tape. Irregularities in film emulsions and in magnetizable materials generate the same problems of accurate reproduction.)

The first phonograph record, in cylindrical shape, was made by Thomas Edison in 1877. The first records in the form of discs were patented in 1896, and the first musical recordings, mostly of operatic stars, began around 1900. These were not serious attempts at recording music, and only featured famous performers, with little regard for musical values. The first serious recordings of symphonic and chamber music occurred in the period from about 1913 to 1919. Phonograph records suffered for a time with the rise of broadcasting, and did not become a significant part of the musical world until electric recording began in 1925. From that time on the phonograph record became a major part of the music industry, and an important matter for performers and the musical public. A long series of technical improvements reached their climax with the long playing record in 1948, and with the subsequent triumph of electronics in conquering or extending the limits of accurate and faithful reproduction of all kinds of music.

Phonograph records have had a major impact on musical life. Many of our symphony orchestras would be forced out of existence were it not for the royalties they receive on the sale of their recordings. On the other hand recordings have replaced musicians at countless practical occasions and have consequently limited severely the number of musicians who can earn their living as musicians. Few dance halls, wedding parties, or broadcasting stations will hire live musicians when a few phonograph records will take their place at a fraction of the musicians' salary. The total effect of the phonograph has been to enrich a small number of performing artists by the sale of records and to force out of the field the great majority.

HIGH FIDELITY

Almost all the problems of accurate recordings either have been eliminated by the ingenuity of technologists or brought near to the vanishing point. And yet we notice that manufacturers and users of records are never satisfied and are continually striving to make recordings ever more vivid, but that something always eludes them.

What eludes them is something that can not be captured by the furthest possible extension of technical improvements: *immediacy.* No matter how much a piece of music is an artifice, no matter how much premeditated thought has gone into its making, its most essential ingredient is its immediate life and spontaneity. No two performances are ever the same, for which we can be thankful. We have emphasized earlier the structural side of music, its architecture. But this is an architecture which is unfolded by the expenditure of living energy, and this expenditure is not a regrettable accident or an external circumstance, but is essential to the music, which has not only intellectual foundations but also organic foundations. Music as an art is closely related, in this respect, to such arts as the drama, poetry, and the dance. The energy of living persons must be expended for these arts to be manifested, and they are far removed from the arts of painting and sculpture which need no performances once a work is completed.

The vogue of the phonograph record is, in this respect, closely related to the current interest in electronic musical instruments, and to the idea of composing by electronic devices. This interest seems to be an attempt to eliminate the human organism and even the human mind and feelings from the field of music. Electronic instruments are built, apparently, in the hope of eliminating the inaccuracies and irregularities of eyes, ears, and hands, and electronic composing devices are used in what seems to be the ambition to eliminate human personality and feeling from the process of composition.

Such developments are extensions of scientific methods and procedures outside the laboratory. For the scientist, the human organism and its senses, and the mind and feelings, are limitations and hindrances—the sources, as often as not, of error and illusion—and therefore to be eliminated as much as possible from his measurements and computations. But for the artist, as for the human being, they are something else. Scientific procedures which are no doubt a form of basic honesty inside the laboratory, when extended beyond its limits become forces making for the dehumanization of life. In this light, one knows how to evaluate electronic instruments and electronic methods of composition, and one can feel only pity for their proponents. It may be remarked that the idea of impersonal composition is not new, and a device—the *arca musarithmica*—a music box for composing, was described at least as far back as 1660. The box contained wooden slides, upon which were written numbers corresponding to the notes of the scale, along with signs for rhythm. By various combinations of the slides, music could be composed in all the classic meters and modes, and "so infinite are the permutations and combinations that, if an angel had begun to combine the numbers at the beginning of the world, he would not have finished today." . . .* No doubt; neither would he have produced any music worth hearing, and we may know in advance what to expect of modern attempts to compose by electronic methods and by modern computers. One can only hope that the public will not be deceived by the proponents of this dehumanization, even though their work bears all the marks of a triumphant ideology.

But it remains to evaluate the phonograph record as a musical tool. We know that its impact on the profession has not been beneficial to the performer. It might be maintained that this defect is compensated for by the widespread diffusion of works of music into homes and areas that would otherwise have no opportunity to hear good music. This is perhaps true, but it is by no means proven that the widespread diffusion of records has led to any rise in musical standards or in the perceptions of the public. Indeed, insofar as phonograph records have made music into a process of passive listening, they have helped to lower the standards, and while they do permit the study and exploration at leisure of large and complex works which are only rarely performed, they also make it possible to ignore such works; it is not yet permitted to read, write, or converse in the concert hall. And even the one virtue which recordings

* Quotation from Athanasius Kircher, "Arca Musarithmica" in George Grove, *Dictionary of Music and Musicians*, edited by Eric Blom, 5th ed., I, 190 (New York, 1954).

might claim with most right, that the performances of great artists need not be lost forever, is in doubt. By chance, the artists we would most like to hear, Bach at the organ, Beethoven, Mozart, Chopin, and Clara Schumann at the piano, Joachim and Paganini on the violin, were not the products of a technological age, and are not available for recording. And even in our own time we have seen many a recording of a work conducted or performed by the composer himself disappear from the record catalogues, replaced by a newer version. Furthermore, some doubts have been raised concerning the stability (over long periods of time) of the plastic materials of which records are made. We may note that our scholars have discovered that the handmade manuscripts and parchments of past eras have endured much longer than modern manufactured paper, which crumbles within a century, and many a scholarly book printed as little as sixty years ago has had to be withdrawn from use by libraries. The paper on which Bach wrote his music is in much better condition today than many a modern edition of his works. The products of technology, like technology itself, have not been with us long enough to demonstrate their capacity to endure over long periods of time.

The technique of tape recording, which permits great flexibility in editing recorded music, has also given rise to a grave abuse: that of splicing together segments of one performance with segments from others. Thus, the artist or engineer who finds the performance of the second or third page of a work unsatisfactory can simply make another tape recording, and replace the defective segment. It is said that many recorded performances today are the composites of many different tape recordings. Recorded music has thus been debased to the level of forgery.

Perhaps another error perpetuated by recordings is that of offering the standards of the virtuoso performer as the only acceptable professional standards. There is such a thing as lifeless perfection, and many performers have achieved it. We should recall the great number of masterworks written for amateur performers, or for professional musicians who probably would not meet our standards. Most masterworks, the Beethoven and Mozart quartets not least among them, first saw the light of day in amateur performances of rather imperfect character, often enough arranged for whatever ensembles could be gotten together. Such conditions are healthy for musical life. The phonograph is at best an adjunct to living music, not a substitute for it. Its real value is in familiarizing the listener with a work for its next concert performance and, for the musician, in preparing himself by studying the performances of great artists.

CHAPTER 10

Listening to Music

Folk music and popular music need no explaining. Their melodies—many of them excellent within the limits they set—are simple, spontaneous, and direct. They express certain feelings and evoke them directly in the listener. But the listener who turns to a quartet of Haydn or Brahms, or to a symphony of Mahler, finds an experience of a different order. There may be moments when a good tune appears, but the moments are few and far between; he finds the composition too long and too complicated.

If he decides that the lack is in himself and not in the music, he may think that he needs to acquire certain information, and so may seek to find out something of the composer's biography, perhaps, or of his personality, or he may seek information about the kind of composition which he has heard, its style and structure.

None of this is necessary or helpful; in fact, it diverts him from his goal. Everything he needs to know is in the sound itself, and no reference to anything else will help. What the listener needs is repeated and attentive listening, in a certain frame of mind.

There are two stages of listening to music, *passive,* and *active.* In the first stage, the sound of the music is enjoyed purely as a sensory process, quite comparable to smoking tobacco or drinking a glass of wine. The listener has no task other than that of making himself passive and sensitive to the flow of sound.

Gradually, the listener can't help noticing a few details, and noticing that certain details are repeated—perhaps the sound of an instrument, a particular melody, or some rhythmic pattern. Even at a first hearing the listener will notice details being repeated. Sooner or later he realizes that something is going on in the music, and he may want to discover, or even take pleasure in discovering, just what is going on.

The process of discovering what is going on in the music is not something technical or complicated. It is a process of memory and comparison, of comparing what one is hearing now with what has gone before in the composition and it is a process of expectation, of learning to anticipate from what goes on now, just what will occur next. At any given moment one hears only some fleeting details, and from these one gradually acquires the ability to conceive the context. It is the listener's task to recognize the form from what he has heard. To do this, he needs only the most primitive perceptions. It was said of General Grant that he was so unmusical that he could recognize only two melodies—one of them was "Yankee Doodle," and the other was not. But just this primitive ability supplies all that the listener needs; the ability to recognize when one is hearing "something" and when one is hearing "something else." At any given moment in a composition, the listener will hear both repetition and change; the beginning of recognizing any musical form consists of recognizing what is the same and what is different. This process goes on in all music, and this ability exists in everyone.

The two forces at work in all music are consistency and variety, identity and change; different musical forms merely show us the different ways these forces operate. In a theme with variations, variety acts to transform the musical substance without touching its essential consistency. Each variation is a definite shape in its own right, yet we recognize its consistency with the theme. In sonata form, the action of these forces is shown in the opposition of two different tonal centers; finally the two are combined and reconciled. A sonata generally exhibits a grouping of themes about two different tonal centers (the so-called first and second subjects of textbook analysis). The melody of one section may be stated in the rhythm of another, or its rhythm may unfold the tones of the other section. In polyphonic music the same material is presented in continually varying juxtapositions. In a chaconne or passacaglia, the same material is repeated over and over again, usually in the lowest part, and it is the task of the upper voices to introduce the element of variety.

This interplay may occur on several levels at the same time; one theme may follow another and yet be part of the same structure, like protagonists who come and go while the scene remains the same; or, the musical scenery itself may change—this we call a change of key or of texture.

It does not require much by way of memory and comparison to understand and enjoy a simple popular tune; what occurs at a given moment is usually in very clear symmetry with what has gone before, and the recognition of this symmetry gives a certain limited pleasure. But the relationships between the different parts of a large symphony are much more extended, and it requires a more careful and attentive faculty of listening and remembering to recognize these relationships. The ear, however (or, more accurately, the mind), has a remarkable ability to grow and extend its capacities, but this growth occurs only with repeated listening and with the thoughtful, active remembering and comparison of the events of the composition.

In the final stage of listening, the listener perceives the concrete shape of the composition (this is not its analytic structure); he has retraced the process by which it was created. He perceives the music as a structure, a coherent succession of rhythmic and tonal relationships.

In making the transition from passive to active listening, it may be well to warn the reader of certain possible errors. Sound itself makes a certain impact upon the nervous system and consequently upon the feelings. Sound is a sensory avenue we cannot close off; we can shut our eyes, but not our ears. The newborn individual hears before he sees, and probably nothing symbolizes the chaos and the power of the universe as does the stream of sound. We are continually engaged in understanding the sounds we hear by relating them to what goes on about us, but let us hear a sound which we cannot immediately relate to some familiar agent about us, and we grow startled and apprehensive. A composition presents us with a continual flow of sounds we do not know very well, and they do make an impact upon the nerves. Also, the motions of music often suggest motions in nature—leaps, gestures, and so on—and may suggest analogies with light and darkness, and all kinds of associations. The listener may think that his nervous responses and his associations with the music are the meaning and the purpose of the music, and so may be diverted from active listening.

A great deal of music has been written which seeks to portray specific things and to evoke them in our imaginations—sadness, gaiety, storms, battles, clouds, wind and waves, and many others—but most of these compositions have fallen by the wayside as mere tricks; very few have achieved any musical value. It remains the listener's task to set aside the play of his feelings and imagination, and to seek to grasp the form of a piece solely by what he has heard.

It is true that there are feelings expressed in the music, which are not just the feelings and associations that each listener brings, more or less accidentally, to the music. Many a test has shown that one and the same composition will arouse very different responses in different persons, even to the point where two persons will attribute to the same piece such opposite emotions as joy and sadness. The music is not responsible for these accidental reactions. The feelings that have entered into the creation of the music, and that are genuinely part of it, are of a different order. They have entered the music as part of the labor of creating it and are accessible only through comprehending that creation.

WHAT IS MUSIC ABOUT?

There have been many attempts to explain the "meaning" and significance of music, none of which appears satisfactory to everyone. It is perhaps impossible to say what music is about. But we might recall our earlier description of music as a dimension added to something else. Music, we have said, originates as the immediate utterance of heightened psychic and physical vitality, and later becomes the means of recalling and evoking these states.

It is, then, clearly akin to play, which in its way, also expresses exuberance and heightened energy; but the very appearance of an activity which is, so to speak, disinterested, in the sense that it is not motivated by any necessity other than the wish to play, indicates the rising of the human mind above necessity into freedom, and in art, as in such related activities as games, rituals, rites, and customs, new forces are set in action upon the mind and feelings. A work of music is an expression of a very general and free contemplation, without specific objects other than the musical materials at hand, and it is only because the work has been so undertaken that it acquires its force and its beauty. It is the product both of contemplation and of the creative action that goes hand in hand with it, working upon a material medium. It expresses states—one would say of soul and spirit had not these words fallen out of the language—that are not reducible to specific terms or specific events. The state of mind may be in some way related to the real world and to the artist's experience of it, but cannot be reduced to some definite cause or event in the artist's life. It is possible that the highest faculties and perceptions of men unfold only in activities, like the arts, that are not occasioned by some practical necessity.

We cannot say "what music is" because there is no language more intimate or immediate to which it could be reduced. It is certainly impossible to say where in our experience of music the physical ends and the subjective begins. No sooner do we hear a melody or a motive than we feel its character and its inherent tendencies, and just as immediately do we become conscious of its place in a structure, unclear though that may be. Music presents us with a continual transition from the sensory to the intelligible; sounds are conveyed to us by a stream of life, and are received by a consciousness that is continually enlarged and clarified. This is not something complex to perform; it is a series of perceptions, so immediate and intimate that they cannot be expressed in language.

The region to which music brings us, which is at once both a matter of organic feeling and of conscious awareness, is one to which most of us have limited access; the creative figures of music have lived in this region more or less as their natural element, and by means of their works permit us to enter it also, as far as we are able to do so.

It has long been perceived that not everything in art is the outcome of consciousness, that an unconscious force must be linked to conscious activity and that it is the perfect unanimity and interpenetration of the two which produces the highest art. Works which lack this seal of unconscious science are recognizable by the palpable absence of a life which is autonomous and independent of their creator, while, on the contrary, where it is in operation, art simultaneously imparts to the work, with the greatest lucidity of the intelligence, that unfathomable reality by virtue of which it resembles a work of nature.*

It is this which gives to works of music—or at least, some of them—their significance, and renders continually interesting even those works which have long been familiar; thus, the work is more than a puzzle or problem which, once solved, offers no further interest. These works are models of the universe and of its life, and therefore of inexhaustible significance.

ON WHAT WORKS OF MUSIC TO LISTEN TO

It might be best for the music lover to attend concerts without knowing what is to be played, just as it would be best for the listener to regard all works as of anonymous authorship and of uncertain date. Sooner or later he will hear a work which makes an impression upon him. He should then seek to explore it further, perhaps by buying and listening to recordings of it, or by trying an arrangement of it for the piano (the publishing of arrangements of large

* Quoted from Friedrich Wilhelm Joseph von Schelling, "Concerning the Relation of the Plastic Arts to Nature" (1807), translated by Michael Bullock, in Herbert Read, *The True Voice of Feeling—Studies in English Romantic Poetry*, p. 331 (New York, 1953).

works for smaller combinations is an important channel of communication between composer and public). He will have no concern for the status of the work or its composer, just as he will assume of those works which fail to impress him that their failure to do so is as likely to be a sign of his unformed perceptions as of a lack in the work. A composition may not be profound but neither may the listener's capacities; many a work that has seemed harsh and perplexing at first hearing has revealed its beauties only through repeated listening.

The listener is forced to trust himself to the concert life available to him, poor as it is. This concert life functions, or should function, more or less as a museum: a place where masterpieces are preserved and exposed to the public. But, as we all know, the functioning of our musical museums—symphony orchestras, opera houses, and so on—is seriously impaired and distorted both by their precarious financial condition and by the subordination of musical values to the dictates of critics, public, and entrepreneurs, all of which forces them to emphasize a very narrow repertoire of masterpieces mixed with works which can only be described as popular and nothing more.*

The listener should also seek to attend performances of contemporary music as much as possible. Even though only a small fraction of what he hears will be of lasting value—like the literary productions of his age—he will not be wasting his time. He will not only help to establish the broken communications between contemporary artists and their publics, but will also be learning something of the evolution of the musical language of his own time, things which are to be found even in compositions of ephemeral worth.

Both types of musical museum—those which preserve the works of past eras which continue to speak to the generations after their

* The desperate condition of our musical institutions has been well described elsewhere. The reader who wishes to know more of this would do well to explore such documentations as Cecil Smith's *Worlds of Music,* Virgil Thomson's *The State of Music,* Archibald T. Davison's *Protestant Church Music in America,* among many others.

own and those which serve as forums for the work of one's own generation—urgently require not merely financial stability, but artistic autonomy as well. Until this happens, music in this country will remain an exotic import only half understood, and of doubtful vitality.

There may be many persons without access to concerts or to those radio stations—if any—in the country which offer good musical programs, who will be forced to rely upon the phonograph record, if they cannot find or help create a musical life in their own community. One can only suggest the purchase of some history of music—almost any one will do—and suggest the opening up at random to almost any portion of the book, except those portions dealing with the music of the past fifty years. These books will offer accurate estimates of the important artists of past generations (except for those few books still about which assume that music history began with Bach; such books are, happily, dying out. It is only in discussing the works of their own time that histories of music falter, and falter very badly; they will safely inform the reader who the great figures were, and are likely to mention those of their works that are especially significant, or which have especially appealed to the authors. It is thus easy to learn of many masterpieces worth hearing. The important thing is to confront any work to be heard without regard to external matters—especially without regard to historical considerations, the century of the work, its country, the influences it exhibits, or the influences it has exerted upon other works. These are of interest to the scholar, but are sterile with regard to the work as art. They are acquired information rather than musical experience, and miss that which renders the work significant: its creation of an autonomous world. Free of such misconceptions, the listener will find his musical perceptions steadily growing, and with this growth his ability to gain access to this world.